MODIGLIANI

MODIGLIANI

by

Claude Roy

SKIRA

RIZZOLI
NEW YORK

© 1985 by Editions d'Art Albert Skira S.A., Geneva

Published in the United States of America in 1985 by

Rizzoli INTERNATIONAL PUBLICATIONS, INC.

597 Fifth Avenue/New York 10017

Reproduction rights reserved by A.D.A.G.P. and
S.P.A.D.E.M., Paris, and Cosmopress, Geneva

The text by Claude Roy was first published
in 1958 in the Skira series "The Taste of Our Time"

Library of Congress Cataloging-in-Publication Data

Roy, Claude, 1915-
    Modigliani.

    Includes index.
    1. Modigliani, Amedeo, 1884-1920.   2. Painters–
Italy—Biography.   I. Title.
ND623.M67R63   1985   759.5   [B]   85-42922
ISBN 0-8478-0630-8

Printed in Switzerland

Contents

6

A life story is never a neat deduction from the apparent facts. Often it seems to fly in the face of facts.

Legend, history's slightly bemused accomplice, has made us familiar with the life story of Amedeo Modigliani. Thus it is common knowledge nowadays that he was born in Italy, at Leghorn, on July 12, 1884; that his childhood and youth were spent at Leghorn, Florence, Rome, Naples, Capri and Venice successively; that in 1906 he came to Paris, where he set order in his art, and disorder in his life; that in the decade beginning 1909 he built up an œuvre and meanwhile wrecked his health; and that he died in the Charity Hospital on January 25, 1920, bled white by work and poverty, by illness, drink and drugs.

Such are the bare facts. Their accuracy is vouched for by birth and death certificates, by correspondence and by his friends' eyewitness accounts.

But let us imagine a biographer who, wishing to trace the career of Modigliani, had only his works to go on; who had to infer the artist's life story solely from internal evidence supplied by paintings, sculptures and drawings; who knew nothing whatever of the facts set forth above; and who had to deduce the course of Modigliani's life from its successive fruits and nothing else. We may be fairly certain that a writer starting from these premises would plot out a life line for Modigliani diametrically opposed to the course it actually took.

For example, on studying the very earliest pictures he would discover in them French, distinctively Parisian influences. Not knowing the young artist's nationality and birthplace, he would naturally assume that Modigliani was a native of the Paris of Toulouse-Lautrec and Cézanne, when

Self-Portrait, 1919. Oil.

7

the recent revelation of African statuary and the first Fauve and Cubist pictures were providing younger, forward-looking artists with new, wildly exciting models, and stimulating them to orgies of originality. The feverish unrest of Modigliani's first canvases, the abruptness of their style, that vehement striving for *expression* at all costs which is evident in (among other works) *The Jewess* and the portraits of Diego Rivera and Frank Haviland, might well lead an observer lacking documented knowledge of their background to picture the artist as a young man who deliberately yielded to the fevers and frenzies of an artistic temperament run wild; who burnt out his days and nights in spasms of sensual pleasure and complete despair.

Then he would watch the painter gradually acquiring self-control, finding himself, working out a personal style and attaining a harmony, a spacious peace, of which there had been no promise in the extravagances of his hectic youth. Thus our detached observer could easily convince himself that, as time went by, Amedeo Modigliani settled down to an ever calmer, more contemplative way of life; that the leaping fires of early youth had burnt themselves out and given place

Portrait of a Young Man Sitting, 1901.
Oil.

Two Women in a Café and Three Studies of Heads,
c. 1906-1909. Pen, ink, watercolor on blue gray paper.

Portrait of Aristide Sommati, c. 1908.
Charcoal on wrapping paper.

to a tranquil radiance. After a stormy début, he had effected, stage by stage, a gradual reconciliation with the creative turmoil of his personality, with other men and with the scheme of things. Our author would picture Modigliani spending his last four years of life in some haven of repose, sheltered from the turbulence and tempests of his adolescence, and giving himself up to musings on the problems of his art and evocations of the flawless faces that haunted his waking dreams. Nor, given the nature of these last creations, would he be over-bold in assuming that Modigliani now had renounced the influences and excitements of his Parisian phase, and had at long last *organized* his life, so as to get the best and most out of it.

Indeed it would be possible, on the strength of certain indications, to maintain the theory that Modigliani must have been leading a sequestered life at this time in the neighborhood of Florence, maybe in some country cottage on the slopes of Fiesole or in the valley of the Mugello, getting up at dawn and going to bed at nightfall, eating simple, wholesome meals washed down with spring water. It would also seem highly probable that now and again Modigliani left his retreat and passed enchanted hours gazing at the pictures of the Sienese and Florentine masters in the Uffizi. For it was

9

Maud Abrantes Writing in Bed, 1908. Pencil. *Mario Buggelli, 1907. Charcoal and pencil on paper.*

now to Simone Martini, to Pisanello, perhaps to Botticelli also, that he looked for guidance. After being born in Paris and passing his formative years in the atmosphere of bold experimentation which was then peculiar to that city, Modigliani—without forgetting what he had seen and learnt in his native France—became aware that Italy, his adopted country, was for him the promised land, the one under whose limpid skies he could best fulfill his destiny. The pictures painted in 1920 testify to his belated—and how rewarding!—discovery of Italy. When he made the portraits of the young woman "Madame J. H." (probably a Florentine) whose face recurs so often in his paintings of the years from 1918 to 1920, he seems often to associate with the direct homage he pays her delicate beauty another, subtler homage to the country of his choice. Thus in one of the portraits of "Madame J. H." he reproduces the movement of the Virgin's hands in Simone Martini's *Annunciation*, in the Uffizi; a sinuous movement whose rhythm he merely reverses, making his sitter's left hand toy with the collar of her sweater just as the Virgin's right hand lightly clasps the border of her hood. (We find much the same movement in Pisanello's *Madonna and Child*, at Verona.)

After observing, as is indeed self-evident, that the last years of the painter's life were marked by a serenity, a harmony, and a pensive, aristocratic detachment which affiliate these works to those of the more contemplative early

Italian masters—after duly noting these facts, our undocumented but perceptive amateur historian might be led to speculate on the reasons for the artist's untimely end. The explanation would surely have to be an *accident*, some brutal impact from outside that abruptly cut short the career of a man who, after successfully weathering the storms of an unruly youth, had settled down in his thirties to a well-regulated life, "all passion spent."

In short our imaginary author would think up a life of Modigliani that was at once highly plausible and completely false, refuted in every detail by the authenticated facts.

For while it sometimes happens that an artist's work tallies with his life, oftener than not they react against each other, the *No* of destiny is challenged by the *Yes* of the creative will. Amedeo Modigliani lived dangerously and disastrously; he disdained, or refused, to put into his way of living the constructive genius he put into his painting. The more ragefully he tore to shreds the fabric of his life, the more strictly he tightened up the fabric of his art; and he devoted as much zeal to self-destruction as to the construction of his talent. He called on that Veronica's veil, the art of painting, to portray the counter-image of the man he was destroying in a passion of despair, and in following the road to ruin achieved his consummation as an artist. His life was a long-drawn suicide, his art the unwearying conquest of a poignant immortality.

The "life story" of Modigliani, the man, does little to explain the achievement of the artist of that name. There were two men within him; this is true to some extent of all of us, but an idiosyncrasy of genius is often the capacity for stepping up to the highest degree this basic antinomy of a human soul.

Amedeo died in an atmosphere of sound and fury, in a mood of anger and despair. But already, long before his death, he had won a high place in the realm of the Voices of Silence and "saved his soul alive."

A Narrow Road in Tuscany,
c. 1898. Oil.

Vita Brevis

"THEY say my age is thirty," Baudelaire noted in his Diary. "But assuming I've always lived three minutes in one, wouldn't my age be ninety?"

Amedeo Modigliani died of pneumonia when he was thirty-six; yet we have a feeling he had lived a century and more.

He was the fourth child in a middle-class Jewish family resident at Leghorn. The loose translation of an Italian word has led to the belief that his father, Flaminio Modigliani, was a well-to-do banker. Actually he was a small businessman who was all but ruined in 1884, the year his last son was born. He ran a *banco*, i.e. a broker's office, but to make ends meet dealt in coal and hides as well.

In the previous generation, however, the Modigliani family had been wealthy. Amedeo's grandfather had lent a large sum to a cardinal of the Roman Curia—a transaction on which he prided himself and on the strength of which he ventured to transgress the law forbidding Jews to acquire real estate. But he was obliged to quit the vineyard he had purchased in the neighborhood of Rome at twenty-four hours' notice. (This was a corollary of the traditional view of the Jews as fated to be "wanderers on the face of the earth." Thus they were prohibited from taking root—with the lamentable result that no Jew could settle down for good in any place or become a landowner. A vicious circle.)

Enraged at this high-handed treatment, Amedeo's grandfather left Rome and moved to Leghorn, though it meant severing all connection with the family home (Modigliani is the name of a small town, just south of Rome, from which the family stemmed).

Portrait of a Woman. Pencil.

Amedeo's mother, Eugénie Garsin, belonged to a family of Sephardim Jews who had established themselves at Marseilles. The private diaries owned by Jeanne Modigliani, daughter of Amedeo and Jeanne Hébuterne, give us glimpses of a lively, strong-minded woman, skeptical, cultured, witty, of a Voltairian turn of mind, who was always at odds with a rather lackadaisical husband; also of the difficulties of raising four children, giving them a good education and a hopeful start in life, on a small, precarious income. Amedeo's elder brother, Giuseppe Emanuele, became one of the leaders of the Italian workers' movement and a socialist Deputy. He went into voluntary exile with the coming of Fascism.

It seems that Eugénie Garsin had that special affection for her last-born son which mothers so often lavish on the Benjamin of a family. Also he seems to have been the most delicate of her brood. In her diary we find a revealing query: "Will he be an artist?" Evidently Amedeo was already showing a taste for art. But though he did well in his studies at the Leghorn Liceo, they were often held up by illnesses. In 1895, when he was eleven, he had an attack of pleurisy; and three years later he went down with typhoid fever, with pulmonary complications. After his recovery, his mother set him to study under a Leghorn artist, Micheli, one of the Macchiaioli group. These painters had willingly adopted the name foisted on them by a hostile critic who jeered at their use of patches—

Head of a Young Woman, 1908. Oil.

14

Portrait of the Engraver Weill, c. 1907. Oil.   *Standing Nude, 1908. Oil.*

macchie— of color. (Similarly, in France, the would-be pejorative epithets "Cubist" and "Impressionist" were proudly accepted by the pioneers of those movements.) The achievement of Fattori, Lega and Signorini, leading figures of the Macchiaioli, has been eclipsed—rather unjustly, some have thought—by the worldwide renown of their French opposite numbers. Fame and the plaudits of posterity are like a train in which there is not room for many passengers; late-comers at the station are likely to be left behind.

Micheli, Modigliani's first teacher, does not rank high among the group which he entered somewhat belatedly. One of the canvases painted by his young pupil has survived: the portrait of a youth seated on a chair in the cold light of a studio. We cannot gaze at this study with a wholly virgin eye. That is one of the dangers of hindsight; it is hard to resist a temptation to read into these conscientious, fumbling efforts of a tyro a promise of the artist's future genius, the superb portraits of Modigliani's later years. But that would be to misread them.

In 1901 the seventeen-year-old boy had trouble with his lungs again and, leaving Leghorn, visited Florence, Rome, Naples and Capri. Florence made an indelible impression on him and he spent happy hours roaming the great art galleries.

Another attraction of the city was that, as he now discovered, Florence was the headquarters of the Macchiaioli group. He settled there in 1902, enrolling in the School of Fine Arts, but broke his stay in 1903 by a long visit to Venice where, too, he worked for a time at the local art school.

But all the time the young artist was haunted by dreams of Paris. At the beginning of the century there were dozens of European youths like himself who felt that their own country, however glorious its artistic past, cramped their élan. "Denmark's a prison." Their one desire was to escape to the capital of the arts, Mecca of aspiring genius. A young Spaniard named Picasso had made the dream come true; in 1904 Brancusi migrated to Paris and Pascin in 1905. The Spaniard Juan Gris, the Russian Wassily Kandinsky and the Italians, Gino Severini and Amedeo Modigliani, followed suit in 1906.

In that Paris of the early 20th century the shadow of the "post-war period" (as it now is called) already lay, unnoticed, across the threshold. The stage was set, the play three-quarters written, the actors had been engaged. Art historians have written at length about the doings of these young men who, when the curtain went up, were to play the leading roles. Modern researchers have traced their migrations from one point of Paris to another, for they were always, characteristically, on the move. Indeed we can chart, as accurately as the travels of Vasco da Gama or Bougainville, the course steered by Picasso the Conquistador on his voyages across Paris, with

Head of a Woman Wearing a Hat, 1907. Watercolor.

Study for The Jewess, 1907. Watercolor.

16

The Jewess, 1908. Oil.

ports of call in the Rue Gabrielle and Boulevard de Clichy, in the Rue Ravignan and Boulevard Voltaire. We know that Modigliani took lodgings successively in the Rue Caulaincourt and the Rue du Delta, in the Rue de Douai and the Passage de l'Elysée-des-Beaux-Arts. But though the ant-like industry of researchers or the good memories of contemporaries can bring vividly before us the material conditions of Modigliani's early years in Paris, of far more interest is the personality of the young newcomer from Italy and his reaction to the atmosphere of the Paris of eighty years ago.

As regards his physical appearance in this period, we know that his height was slightly below the average; that he gave an impression of being always on his toes, both physically and mentally, eager to charm by asserting his personality and to assert his personality by dint of charm. Zadkine has well described the singular attractiveness of this dark handsome youth. "He had a massive forehead topped by a dark cloud of hair, black and glossy as a raven's plumes, a cleanshaven chin, a face of alabaster whiteness dappled with bluish shadows." But, except for a few perceptive friends, those who were then in touch with Modigliani have strangely little to tell us. They knew him no doubt, but quite failed to realize the man they knew was—Modigliani. Whereas already everyone in Montmartre had an inkling that Picasso was—Picasso. The young Italian with an addiction to pretty girls and good poetry struck them as being little more than a talented playboy.

Three Studies for The Horsewoman,
1909. Pencil.

The Horsewoman, 1909. Oil. ▷▷

Something of the young artist's temperament can be gleaned from the letters he wrote around 1900 to his friend Oscar Ghiglia, from the rather precious aphorisms he made a practice of inscribing in the margins of his drawings, from the books his friends saw bulging his pockets or scattered about his studio, and from the verses he had a habit of reciting late at night, intoxicated no less by the verbal imagery of his favorite poets, Dante, Carducci and D'Annunzio, than by the drinks he had imbibed. All alike speak for that poetic vision of the world which Modigliani had developed as an art student in Italy from his contacts with fellow students and from the writers he had learnt to love in early youth.

Nothing becomes more promptly and pathetically out-moded than a period sensibility. Writers who harp on the *mal du siècle* which every century reinvents for itself seem quite unreadable once their period has become ancient history. On modern Italians as on contemporary Frenchmen D'Annunzio produces the impression of a rather turgid rhetorician; we are no less irked by his grandiloquence, his gesturings and boastings than by the affectations of his style. Some time, perhaps, he may return to favor. Only yesterday he thrilled deliciously his reader's nerves—though today he gets on ours!

When, after a long series of humiliations, Italy had lost faith in her destiny, he came forward as priest and poet of a national renascence. Modigliani, like all young Italians of his generation, fell under the spell. And, in his case, admiration for the poet who at the age of fifteen could write the *Canto Novo*, for the author of that stupendous novel *Child of Pleasure*, was enhanced by the fact that he seemed to find in D'Annunzio's work a solution to his own problems. Product of the combined influences of Nietzsche, Walt Whitman, Emerson and Ibsen, that myth of the Superman, so eloquently promulgated by D'Annunzio, must have answered to some of the young artist's personal aspirations. Though it would be rash in Modigliani's case to predicate any "drama of the soul"— hypothetical at best, with so few specific elements to go on —we must not forget that he was an Italian, born at a time when the country was athirst for freedom; that his family had been reduced to poverty; that he was the grandson of a Jew, victim of racial injustice. We can picture Modigliani in his boyhood dazzled by the glorious eloquence of the great Italian poet, puffing out his chest, drawing himself to his full height in an attitude of proud defiance. It was by way of D'Annunzio that he discovered Nietzsche. Those idols of the young men of his day, along with Carducci and Baudelaire,

Head and Bust, c. 1908. Pencil.

Portrait de Doucet   modigliani

22

André Derain (1880-1954):
Portrait of Modigliani.
Lead pencil on white paper.

Portrait of Picasso, c. 1915. Pencil.

◁ *Portrait of André Derain. Pencil.*

opened up a whole new world of hope. We find frequent echoes of them in the impassioned, high-flown verbiage of the young artist's notes and letters. "I see my years to come as a great river overbrimming its banks and flooding all around with joy." Or again: "You shall possess only what you win by force." "I shall forge a cup to serve as a receptacle of my Passion." (Passion with a capital "P", needless to say!)

If we seek a key to the early *attitudes* of Modigliani—but not necessarily to his art—we shall find it in D'Annunzio and Nietzsche. What struck everyone who met him in Montmartre, and afterwards Montparnasse, was not only his distinguished bearing but a tendency to ostentation, carried to the point of aggressiveness, provocative self-assertion, particularly when he was in his cups. He had a taste for showing off his paces, for theatrical effects. Even his drunkenness, as Adolphe Basler has aptly remarked, was "as much demonstrative as natural." And behind his fits of petulance no less than his generous enthusiasms lay, it would seem, a conviction that the creative artist is a privileged being. "We have different rights from other people's," he once wrote to Ghiglia, "because we have different needs, which—and this we must forever believe in and proclaim—set us above the morality of the world at large."

24

A Tragic Generation

MODIGLIANI left Italy when he was twenty-two and afterwards made only relatively brief stays in that country. It was in Paris that his art matured, in Paris that he made the friendships which counted for most in his career, and in Paris that he died.

Nonetheless, if we are to understand the haunted element of his inner life, that frantic urge to self-destruction which ran parallel with an ever-increasing mastery of his artistic means, that tragic ambivalence which led him, while producing works of a sublime serenity, to a course of life not merely dangerous but suicidal—if we are to understand the singular dualism of his personality we must take into account the intellectual climate of his Italian boyhood.

When he was studying art in Florence, where Fattori, then an old man and the most eminent member of the Macchiaioli group, was exercising much influence on the pupils of the School of Fine Arts (where he had been a teacher), Amedeo struck up a friendship with a young writer three years older than himself, Giovanni Papini. Philosophical and literary discussions were the order of the day in Florence, and Papini, a typical representative of the Tuscan intelligentsia, had fallen under the spell of Nietzsche and D'Annunzio. A militant atheist, he turned out articles remarkable for their truculence and turgidity in a forcible-feeble style. Associated with the group and with the many little magazines which cropped up under their auspices, withered and sometimes precariously revived, were several young men whose lives were as tragic as Modigliani's. "Many of them," writes an historian of the period, "ended up by killing themselves, whether outright or, methodically, by slow degrees." It was

The Cellist, 1909. Oil.

in fact a Lost Generation. When we examine the work of what was then known as the "twilight school," the writers contributing to the vanguard magazine *La Voce*, and the Futurists, we find a mixture of pessimism and violence, rage and despair, voiced in very different tones according to their diverse temperaments. Most brilliant of the "Twilight" group was Italo Svevo, a Triestine engineer of Jewish origin, and it included Guido Gozzano who died of consumption at the age of twenty-seven and Sergio Corazzini who died when he was twenty ("I have but my tears," he wrote, "to dedicate to silence"). Carlo Michelstaedter, another Jewish writer, hailing from Gorizia, after publishing some sensationally brilliant articles, killed himself at the age of twenty-three. Scipio Slataper, a young man of the same generation, flung himself into the war as a man flings himself into the sea—to perish in it. Federico Tozzi died in poverty the same year that

Study for The Cellist, 1909. Oil.

Head of a Young Girl. Limestone.

Head of a Woman, 1910. Oil.

Modigliani died in Paris. Dino Campana, anarchist and globe-trotter, who played a brief part in the Futurist movement, died insane. These young men born in the 1880s have been described by a student of the Italian scene as "a tragic generation whose genius drove them to intolerance of life" —often, indeed, to rejection of it.

In short, for the group of Italian intellectuals to which Modigliani belonged, living was no simple matter. Some poems found among his papers after his death have been published. True, Modigliani was a great poet only in his painting; nevertheless these lines have a certain psychological interest as revealing something of the spiritual climate of his brief existence. In one he says he "sheds the tears of those who have failed to reach the stars." Elsewhere, he speaks of listening to "the great soundless tumult in the midnight of the soul."

Coming to Paris from the "twilight" of pessimistic Italy, from a land bathed in the light not so much of the Mediterranean sun as of the black sun of melancholy, and knowing by heart hundreds of lines of the greatest, most forlorn of all

The Beggar of Leghorn, 1909. Oil.

Portrait of a Young Girl, c. 1905. Oil.

Italian poets, Leopardi, Modigliani entered a world where, as in Italy, life was not taken lightly.

Many of those who were young men in that period and outlived it, and most of the writers who have described and glamorized it, seem to have been impressed mainly by its picturesque side, by the frolics and fantasy of its "Bohemian" life, by the Golden Legend of artists who had never gold and rarely silver in their pockets but squandered the treasure of their youth lightheartedly between the rival eminences of Montmartre and Montparnasse. "At the junction of Boulevard Raspail and Boulevard Montparnasse," writes Giraudoux, "we find a strange and wonderful assemblage of Parisianized exotics: Japanese expressionists, Swedish cubists, Icelandic engravers, Turkish medalists, Hungarians and Peruvians with complementary vocations, each attended by a semi-wife with a make-up of her original own, each of them dressed in a manner that would make him pass for crazy in his hometown, yet representing in this part of Paris—even for his concierge—the minimum of eccentricity." But all this colorful variety, this defiant bizarrerie, was no more than froth on the surface of reality, the outward trappings of a dedicated youth. These young men—anyhow the best of them—were not drawn to Paris by the lure of a *vie de bohème*; their minds were steeped in memories of the poets and the outcast painters who had walked the streets of Paris only yesterday, and the names of Baudelaire and Villon, Gauguin and Van Gogh were often on their lips. They were not out (as some imagined) to "startle the bourgeois" or to "have a good time." The drinks and drugs, the frenzy these young artists brought to charging, headlong, at the blind wall of reality —or overleaping it in that wine-flushed delirium which gave wings to Utrillo's and Soutine's imagination and, in Modigliani's case, the hashish-tinged dreams that lifted him above himself into a world of light—all these were not the follies of

Woman with Red Hair, 1915. Oil.

Portrait of Constantin Brancusi, 1909. Oil.
On the back of the study for The Cellist.

youth which, as the saying goes, will have its fling, but indications of a febrile sensitivity wrought up to the breaking-point.

Historical factors and the social climate of the age may seem to account for and throw light on the frantic, distraught energy Modigliani expended on the process of self-destruction. He was blood brother of the "twilight poets," but also heir of those pilgrims of the Absolute whose tragedy is voiced by Baudelaire in *Les Paradis Artificiels*, and here we have, not a *mal du siècle* peculiar to that or any time, but a spiritual unrest not to be accounted for by history and social environment. When Baudelaire wrote *Wine and Hashish compared as Means of Multiplying the Personality*, he did not provide merely the key to his own catastrophe but also, in advance, that of the secret kingdom Modigliani was to enter, never to return. "Man's incorrigible addiction to all the substances, harmless or lethal, that exalt his personality, testifies to his greatness. He is always seeking to exalt his day-to-day existence and to take wing towards the Infinite."

But for Modigliani the painter, as for Baudelaire the poet, only the creative act could lead the way to that total self-realization whose artificial surrogates they sought in drunkenness, in nocturnal adventure, in hashish and excesses of all sorts. That state of grace of which Baudelaire speaks, when the mind seems poised serenely above dejection and disgust —when "the outside world presents itself to him in strong relief, with an amazing sharpness of definition and a wealth of color"—was attained by Modigliani not by way of drugs or the thrills of "scarlet nights" but in solitude and silence, in tranquil contemplation of a canvas or a block of stone. For Modigliani more than for any other, that "true life" of which Rimbaud wrote lay elsewhere—and of this he was supremely conscious. "Clarions of silence," he writes in one of his poems,

"ship of quietude
"lull me
"to sleep
"until the new day dawns."

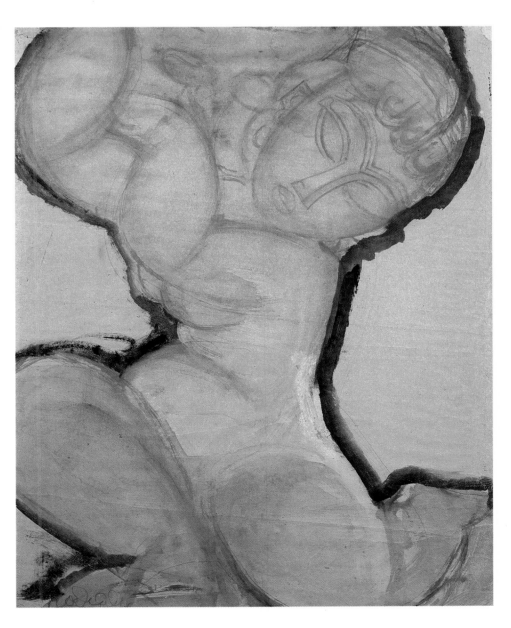

Rose Caryatid with a Blue Border,
c. 1913. Watercolor.

31

Portrait of Jean Alexandre, 1909. Oil.

Three portraits of Dr Paul Alexandre, dated 1909, 1911 and 1913, are spaced out over what were the five crucial years of Modigliani's artistic evolution. In the intervals of painting them he made hundreds of drawings of his friend, studied African and Gothic statuary and himself practised the art of sculpture. The three portraits might be titled:

Prelude, Variation and Fugue on the Theme of a Face.

The first is something of a bravura piece, displaying more virtuosity than originality. The line is elusive, imprecise, and, following Cézanne's technique, the painter relies almost exclusively on color for rendering volume and perspective. Indeed this elegant, sophisticated portrait might have been signed by any one of the five or six most brilliant portrait painters of the day. But from 1910 to 1913 Modigliani laid more and more stress on line, though calling on color (of a much simplified type) discreetly to suggest effects of modeling. He was moving towards an ever greater economy of means. What is so remarkable here is the way in which, while accentuating distortions and progressively simplifying his brushwork, Modigliani succeeds in producing in each case a better likeness, both factually and psychologically. Anyone who, like the present writer, has met Dr Alexandre, cannot fail to be struck by the way in which, in each successive portrait, the model becomes all the more his natural self, the more the painter's creative self comes to the fore.

Portrait of Paul Alexandre
against a Green Background, 1909. Oil.

Portrait of Paul Alexandre, 1911-1912. Oil.

Portrait of Paul Alexandre Before a Window Pane, 1913. Oil.

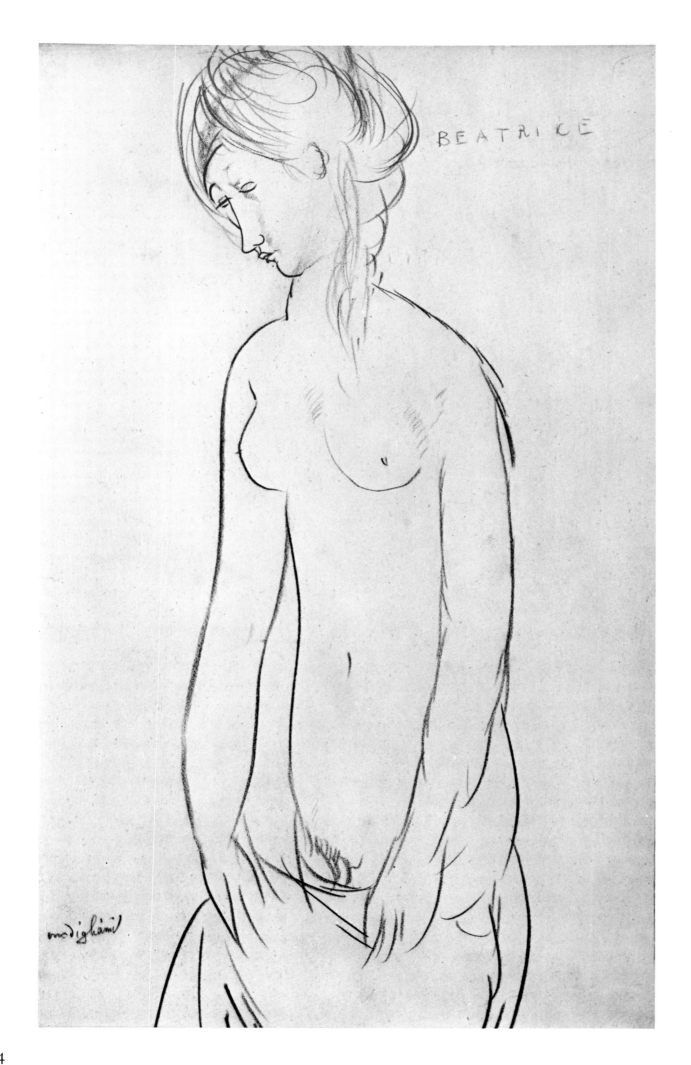

BEATRICE

modigliani

34

A New Day Dawns

THE letters of his youth, the glimpses we get of his early friendships in Italy, the books he read and his favorite poems throw light on the state of mind in which young Modigliani came to Paris late in 1905 or early in 1906. For those who came in contact with him in Montmartre he was only "that young Italian who roamed the streets and ran after the girls." As yet there was no drinking or drug-taking. Full of high seriousness, he claimed to be a fervent admirer of Spinoza, who, according to a family legend, was a forbear of his mother. The Montmartre girls he fell in love with for a day or two and painted for an hour or two attached no more importance to the good-looking young Italian than did his fellow painters, who regarded him as a mere amateur. One of his girl friends explained to André Warnod that she had always dreamed of living with an artist. That was why she left Modi when she finally got a chance of living with an "artiste" —the real thing, a clown at the Cirque Médrano!

By the time Modigliani arrived in Paris and took his first studio in the Rue Caulaincourt, the sculptor Brancusi had been living there for the past year. Another newcomer was Pascin, followed a few months later by Juan Gris and Severini. Matisse had just bought his first Negro statuettes from a curio-dealer in the Rue de Rennes. Cézanne died in October 1906 and in the following year at the Salon d'Automne a large Cézanne retrospective exhibition created a sensation. Picasso was about to set to work on *Les Demoiselles d'Avignon* and a young picture-dealer, D. H. Kahnweiler, also a newcomer to Paris, was planning to open in the Rue Vignon a small art gallery whose mission was to publicize and promote the cause of Cubism.

Beatrice, c. 1916-1917. Pencil.

35

One of Modigliani's first associates, and one of the first to collect his work, was Dr Paul Alexandre. Together they visited the exhibitions of Cézanne and Matisse, the two painters who, with Toulouse-Lautrec and perhaps Steinlen and Boldini, most strongly appealed to Modigliani. In the antique shops, at Paul Guillaume's gallery and at the Ethnographic Museum of the Trocadéro Modigliani's eyes—like those of many others—were opened to the magical art of Negro masks and carvings.

He made friends easily and in many walks of life, yet he remained aloof, something of a lone wolf. He looked on with amusement and interest, but without committing himself, while his Italian friends let off the noisy fireworks of Futurism. Gino Severini tells us how in 1909 he got *No* for an answer when he asked Modigliani to sign the Futurist Manifesto which he and Umberto Boccioni had just drawn up. The Futurists had declared war on the defunctive traditions of Italy—"that land of the dead, an immense Pompeii, white with graves." Vociferously they heaped insults on the museums and reviled "old canvases, old statues, old objects, all that's moth-eaten, grimy, putrefied by time." This program was far from winning Modigliani's approval.

Portrait of Beatrice Hastings, 1915. Oil.

Portrait of a Woman ▷ (Madame Dorival?), 1916. Oil.

37

Portrait of Diego Rivera, 1914. Pen and ink.

Study for the Portrait of Diego Rivera, 1914.

Dr Alexandre remembers how Amedeo used to cover the walls of his studios with reproductions of the Italian masters. Nothing was further from his wishes than to burn down the Louvre or the Uffizi. And in the eyes of many of his comrades, amid the Babel of experiments and topsy-turvy values in that Paris of eighty years ago, he must have cut the figure of a tame conservative, not to say a spineless reactionary.

All the work produced by Modigliani between his arrival in Paris and his return to Leghorn in 1909, before he finally settled in France for good, makes us feel that we have here an artist trying to hit on the right pitch of voice, continually changing registers, never content with the tone adopted, making a series of fresh starts in quest of some vaguely sensed ideal.

But already a basic element of his art was coming to the fore, never to be relinquished, sole constant among many variables. His friends and fellow artists devoted themselves turn by turn to landscape, the more aggressive reconstructing space and disintegrating its elements; to the still life (now that Cézanne had shown the way), which they took to pieces and

Portrait of Frank Burty Haviland, 1914. Pencil.

Portrait of Frank Burty Haviland, 1914. Oil.

reassembled; to the large compositions consecrated by tradition, whose rhythms they revitalized. Not so Modigliani. He concentrated on a single theme, scanned but one horizon, explored but one landscape, pored over a single motif. He was the Oedipus of that obsessive Sphinx: the human face and body.

On the main line of evolution that runs from Cézanne's *Montagne Sainte-Victoire* to Picasso's *Reservoir at Horta de Ebro* it is useless trying to find a place for Modigliani. The three apples, the guitar, the bottle and the newspaper, which had become for modern painting what the top-hat, the wand, the handkerchief, the pigeon and the rabbit are to the conjurer's repertory—these and their derivatives meant nothing at all to Modigliani. His paintings have the exquisite monotony of a lifelong passion. It is an obsession of the mind to which he has given body. Except for a few portraits of couples (*Bride and Groom*, *Lipchitz and his Wife*) and a few of children side by side, he enters into no other relationship than that of the artist alone with his model; he broaches no problem of composition other than that of a single human being viewed face

Portrait of Pablo Picasso, 1915. Pencil.

to face. For Modigliani a landscape or an interior is no more
than a background. We learn nothing of the surroundings in
which his sitters live from day to day, he takes no interest in
that. He does not bring before us period figures whose way
of life is written all over them, as Degas and Lautrec had
done, and as Bonnard (whom he also admired) and Vuillard
still were doing. There is no room in his pictures for accesso-
ries or knick-knacks. Passing by these details, he penetrates
the inner lives of the models before him. The revelation of
Negro and Khmer art, together with the achievements of
Brancusi, and later of Lipchitz, attracted him to sculpture but
they lured him away from none of the essentials of his art.
Modigliani in his chosen field is not a member of that great
family of creators, men like Balzac and Vermeer, Proust and
Bonnard, for whom the everyday world is of primordial importance; who to define a human personality must needs
describe the house the man lives in, the objects he handles, the
mirrors that show him his reflected self, the furniture that is
the décor of his days. Modigliani deliberately disregards what

Portrait of Pablo Picasso, 1915. Oil.

seems to him mere anecdote, the small change of daily life. He paints as Madame de La Fayette, Racine and Benjamin Constant wrote and the backgrounds of his canvases have the allusive terseness of the stage directions in classical tragedy —"Scene: A Palace."

The years during which he was learning to be the Modigliani we know are a long chronicle of renunciation and purification, a ceaseless stripping away of everything incidental and accidental in the spirit and substance of his art. When we examine the works covering the period 1905-1913, we are tempted to share that patient impatience which led the painter to overcome, one by one, the successive temptations afforded by the study of other masters, and to make haste to reach that stage of his career in which superficial observers thought he had hit on a manner, whereas in reality he had achieved a style. The young artist who combined the crispness of Lautrec's line with Cézanne's volumetric construction and the nervous vehemence of the Fauve palette to paint the well-nigh expressionist *Portrait of a Jewess* and the two versions of

Madam Pompadour, 1915. Oil.

Self-Portrait as Pierrot, 1915. Oil.

Mateo Alegria, 1915. Brush and ink wash.

Bride and Groom, 1915-1916. Oil.

Portrait of Henri Laurens, 1915. Oil.

Portrait of Max Jacob, 1916. Oil.

The Cellist was not yet *our* Modigliani. Nor was it he who in the *Standing Nude* of 1908 exploited all the resources of the physical properties of oils, with a lavish impasto molded in relief and punctuated by lighter brushstrokes to make the girlish body sing its siren song. It was not yet *our* Modigliani who painted the very early portraits of Dr Alexandre, so curiously reminiscent of Whistler. And though the admirable *Portrait of Brancusi* on the back of one of the *Cellists*, sketched and then rejected by the artist, brings us face to face with the tectonic dynamism of a great painter, it does not as yet give any intimation of his ultimate developments.

46

Modigliani and Sculpture

THERE is a missing link, probably a vital one, in the evolution of Modigliani's art. It is on record that in 1909 he met Constantin Brancusi. In the autumn of that year he returned to Leghorn, probably under pressure of financial straits and the necessity of recruiting his health, already undermined by the abuse of alcohol and drugs, lack of sleep and undernourishment. We know that, warmly encouraged by Brancusi, he worked hard at sculpture during that stay in Italy. There is reason to believe that he even visited the marble quarries at Carrara. What we know for certain, however, is that all the statues made in 1909 were "drowned" in a canal at Leghorn by the artist himself. Modigliani was subject to these moods of iconoclast destructiveness. Even before that, in a fit of drunken fury in Paris, he had destroyed the work of several of his friends in a studio in the Rue du Delta. This time it was on himself that he vented his rage. Presumably he had shown his work to some brother artists at Leghorn and they had disapproved of it. Modigliani took a hand-cart, loaded it with all the pieces of sculpture he had been working on, and dumped them *en bloc* into the nearest canal.

Later, back in Paris, Modigliani reverted to sculpture several times. There can be no doubt that he was constrained to abandon a very promising career as a sculptor for purely material reasons. This is not to say that he fell back on painting and drawing simply as a makeshift, or that he reluctantly practised these arts while pining for the hammer and chisel. But it was unquestionably his experience of sculpture that enabled Modigliani to discover and develop his true means of expression.

Head, 1911-1913. Limestone.

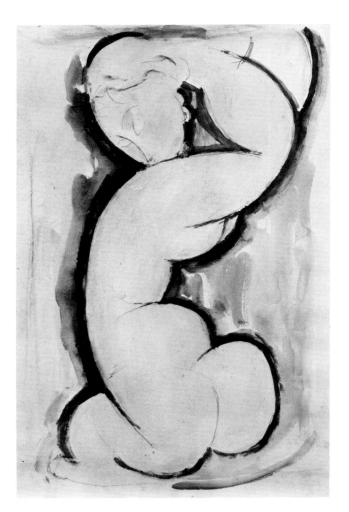

Green Caryatid, c. 1913. Gouache.

Caryatid. Watercolor.

By 1909 he had left the Right Bank and settled in the Cité Falguière, in Montparnasse. It was there that the sculptor Jacques Lipchitz made his acquaintance. Lipchitz has given a description of one of his visits to Modigliani's studio in the spring or summer of that year. He found him working out-of-doors. Some five stone heads were placed on the ground in front of the studio. Modigliani was trying them out in various combinations, since, as he explained to his friend, they were intended to figure together, as a group. So far as Lipchitz can remember, these heads were exhibited at the Salon d'Automne, arranged in order of height like organ pipes, "as if to suggest a secret melody that was running in their creator's mind."

During the long discussions that took place in Brancusi's studio, Modigliani gradually convinced himself that Rodin had been leading sculpture along the road to ruin. He stigmatized the practice of modeling in clay as a perversion, a fruitless manipulation of "mud" that could only result in works devoid of vigor and grandeur. In vain did Lipchitz

48

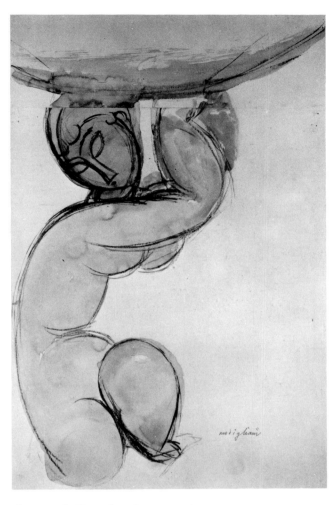

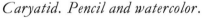
Caryatid. Pencil and watercolor.

Caryatid, 1913. Oil.

àrgue that the mere act of carving directly in the stone was not enough *per se* to generate style and power, that in the hands of a great artist the softest stone, even clay and plaster of Paris, can be given all the hardness and austerity of marble; nothing would cure Modigliani of his fixed idea. It is only fair to add, however, that in the case of Modigliani this fixation on a single technique merely reflected a single-minded pursuit of a clearly apprehended plastic ideal.

When we cast round for referents in terms of which that ideal might be clarified, we think immediately of Negro art and the first modern works that Modigliani must have seen and studied, those of Nadelmann, Lehmbruck and Brancusi. But other correspondences suggest themselves. It may be granted that Modigliani followed the example of certain African schools in systematically elongating faces, in treating neck and throat almost as geometrical figures, in playing off the curved outlines of a face against the sharply defined rectilinear volume of the nose, and in so doing displayed all the boldness of the Negro mask-carvers. Yet it is impossible not

Caryatid, c. 1913-1914. Pastel and watercolor over a pencil drawing.

Caryatid, c. 1915. Pencil and watercolor.

Caryatid, c. 1914. Limestone.

to feel that he had also pondered over the archaic art of the Greeks, over Khmer sculpture and Gothic statuary. Surely it is the smile of the Greek *Korés*, of the statues of Angkor and Reims, that plays on the lips of the *Smiling Head*

It may truly be said of Modigliani—as indeed of the greatest artists of his time—that in his pursuit of a style he took his lead not from the Greece of early times, not from Africa, not from the East, not from medievaldom, but from that sixth continent of the art world: Archaia.

Here Archaia designates that Golden Age, that ideal archaic past in which our present-day sensibility—with willful but fruitful blindness—confounds a medley of aspirations and achievements which, as the specialist well knows, cannot be placed on the same footing, compared or contrasted with each other without the risk of misconstruing them. Very likely this Archaia is no more than an optical illusion. But we have learned that every illusion of the eye has its origin in a compulsion of the mind, and that before seeing what actually is, we see what we wish and *need* to see.

The modern zest for exploration of hitherto uncharted regions of the globe, the successive discoveries of archeologists, the uncovering of objects hidden for centuries underground, all this sufficiently explains the brusque emergence of a number of ancient works and schools, and the keen interest suddenly focused on them. When explorers and conquerors bring back from *terrae incognitae* the relics of civilizations of which nothing formerly was known, obviously there is nothing essentially subjective about these resuscitations of lost or prehistoric arts.

All the same, the buried treasure of ancient cultures can never manifest itself to us as a balanced, coherent whole, it cannot be taken in at a glance or appraised with unbiased eyes. Sometimes we have the works of the past before us, but to no avail: our sensibilities are not yet attuned to them. We look at them uncomprehendingly; sometimes indeed we flatly refuse to see them. Thus at a time when most of Africa had already been explored, when its fetishes and statuettes were already amply represented in our museums, Negro statuary was considered beneath the notice of anyone but specialized students of primitive cultures. This state of scrupulous, self-inflicted blindness was epitomized by Louis XIV who, when shown some Chinese porcelain figures, waved them aside, with the words: "Away with those baubles!" These sentiments were echoed in the eighteenth century by Buffon: "Is not the taste for Chinese grotesques and the cult of idols the very acme of stupidity?"

We find for example that until very recently the study of pre-Columbian art was left entirely to professional historians

Three Studies for Sculptures, 1910-1911.

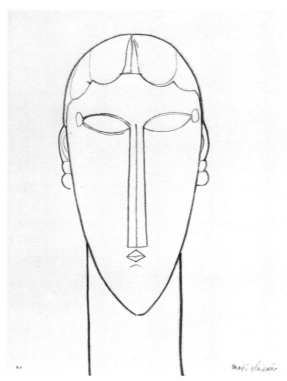
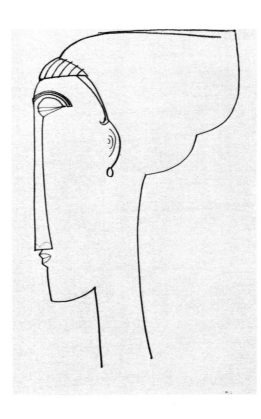

Head. Marble.

Marcelle, 1917. Oil.

and sociologists, and these works were unrepresented in that pantheon of aesthetic sensitivity which André Malraux has named "the Museum without Walls." Yet four centuries have gone by since the emissaries of Cortes were ushered into the presence of Charles V with gifts from the Emperor Montezuma. On the 27th of August 1520, a traveler who was shown them made the following entry in his diary: "Never in all my life have I seen anything that made my heart so leap as did these admirable objects of art." The name of that enraptured observer was Albrecht Dürer. Undoubtedly he was one of the few men of the time to associate those objects with art.

Now when Matisse, Brancusi, Picasso and Modigliani discovered Negro art, most of the objects that fascinated them had been on view in Paris for years. But they were housed in a museum which did not, and was not intended to, arouse the *esthetic* interest of visitors. They formed part of a domain whose subject-matter was dealt with in publications of the *Société de Géographie* and the *Journal des Voyages*, not in the *Gazette des Beaux-Arts* or the *Journal des Arts*.

53

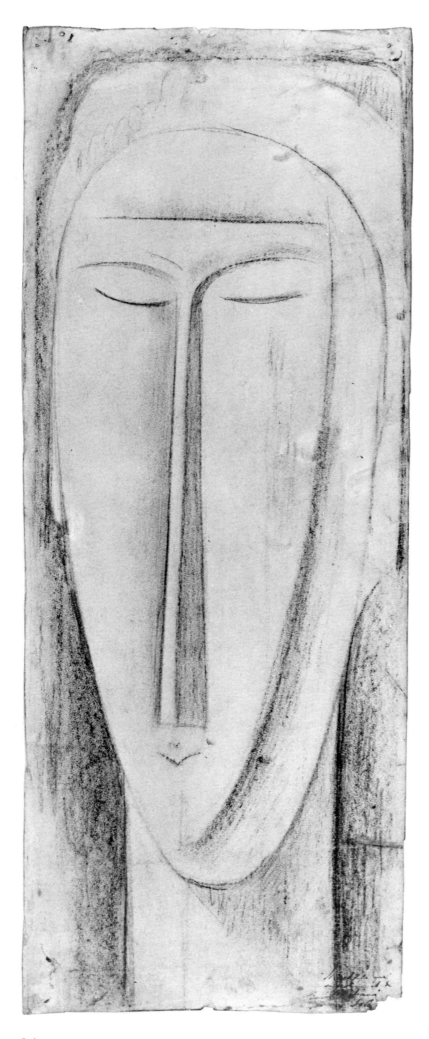

Smiling Head, 1912-1913. Limestone. ▷

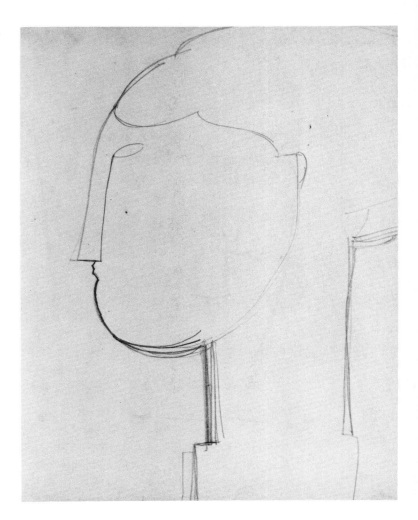

Sheet from a sketchbook, 20 January 1914. ▷
Chalk and pencil.

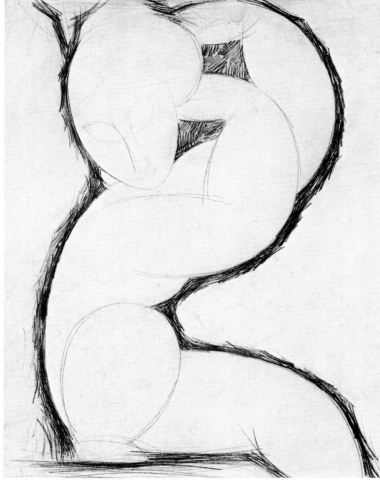

Caryatid , c. 1912-1914. Pencil.

Head. Limestone. ▷▷

Sheet from a sketchbook, 20 January 1914. ▷
Chalk and pencil.

58

Head. Limestone.

Portrait of Beatrice Hastings, 1915. Oil.

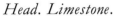

◁ Head, c. 1911-1912. Limestone.

In the same way, when President de Brosses and Stendhal visited the museums of Italy, the pictures that interested Modigliani a century later were already on view. If, in their eagerness to feast their eyes on Raphael and the Carracci, they hurried past the works of Berlinghieri and Simone Martini without noticing them, the reason is not only that they had no eyes with which to see them, but that the Primitives spoke a language to which they were still deaf.

Though modern art chooses its own forbears and eagerly draws inspiration from a fabulous Archaia peopled almost indiscriminately with Sienese Primitives and Pahouin ancestor-statues, archaic Greek sculpture and Celtic artifacts, Sardinian figurines and Gallic coins, nevertheless the example of Modigliani goes far to show that there has not been any real break in our times with what is known as the classical tradition, but only with a simulacrum of it, with the dead forms and stereotyped procedures that once usurped the name of classicism.

When young Modigliani took his cue simultaneously from photographs of the masterpieces of the Italian Renaissance pinned to the walls of his studio and from the Negro carvings he and his friend Dr Alexandre inspected in the museums and antique shops, from statues of Khmer divinities and canvases by Cézanne, he was definitely not (as his Futurist friends loudly claimed to be doing) severing the ties that bound him to that vast corpus of works of plastic art which testify to the immemorial aspiration of the human spirit. His own desire, on the contrary, was to bind those ties securely. What he and his companions did break with—and how drastically!—was Academicism. Turning from its "inspissated gloom," they sought the freer light of that Universal Academy where art is never what meets the eye, where painting and sculpture betoken no passive surrender to the facts of visual experience, but, on the contrary, an heroic conquest of reality by the creative spirit.

For Meissonier and Bouguereau, for the Schools, painting was synonymous with submission to the dictates of optical reality, data that can be recorded only in terms of a strictly prescribed, unalterable grammar. There is, they said, a syntax of nature whose laws it is the artist's duty to abide by. Thus the Ecole des Beaux-Arts drummed into the pupils the sacrosanct laws of proportion and perspective, the golden rule of the "seven and a half heads." Another axiom was that for the problem set by any motif, there was—as in mathematics—only one correct solution, all others being mere aberrations.

The academic fallacy consists in the belief that nature can be copied, that nature provides a paradigm whose every aspect it is the artist's task to reproduce with servile accuracy; and another error of Academicism is that it substitutes the logic of convention for the logic of the thinking mind.

Actually it is not the existence of canons and rules that sterilizes a style or dessicates an art. We know that in the earliest ages the proportions of a painting or a statue were rigidly governed by magico-mathematical rules and that the craftsman's handiwork strictly complied with the forms prescribed by priest or donor. The bane of periods of decadence is that they foster the belief that their arbitrary canons and deliberate distortions have an absolute, intrinsic value; that their conventions are not mere conventions and that the procedures enjoined on the artist have their roots not in the minds of men but in objective laws of nature. The fraud of all Academicisms (for it is nothing short of a fraud) is to pretend that the canons they have formulated are not arbitrary, and that in complying with them the artist does not distort and deform.

When the African sculptor and the Egyptian painter, the Gothic stone-carver and the Primitive abide by a set code of rules regarding the proportions to be given sacred figures and so forth, these rules are constituent elements of a vision of the world that is fundamental to their creative instinct. These imperatives are part and parcel of a system of values which is

Standing Nude Figure ▷
(profile and front views),
c. 1912. Limestone.

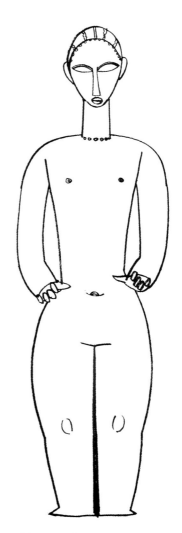

Hermaphrodite, 1910-1911.
Pencil.

60

Study for a Caryatid, c. 1912. Oil.

62

Head of a Woman, c. 1910. Limestone.

Head, c. 1912. Limestone. ▷

Head, c. 1911-1912. Limestone.

Head of a Woman (profile and three-quarter views).
Limestone.

Portrait of Beatrice Hastings, 1915. Oil.

not imposed on the artist from without but to which he willingly subscribes. Distortions and anomalies of perspective all have their place in a self-sufficient hierarchy and a spiritual reorganization of the visible world in which every seeming constraint has its purpose and a profound significance.

When the Renaissance dawned and theological and animistic concepts were superseded by a humanist interpretation of the world, the artist was led to draw up his own rules, to work out a syntax of vision for his personal use, to build up and perfect a well-planned system of relationships. The monk Dionysius began his treatise on painting with a homily: "After praying, the pupil should school himself with accuracy in the proportions and nature of figures." Alberti began his treatise on painting with a sage remark: "Note the manner in which objects enter our field of vision." For the religious painter the canons of painting were the fruit of divine revelation. For the humanist painter they were a victory of the human mind.

Portrait of Beatrice Hastings, 1916. Oil.

But for the academic, as for the decadent painter, there is no question either of a revelation or of a victory. The dogmas of the Ecole des Beaux-Arts are founded neither on sacred authority nor on personal discovery. They represent a body of teachings neither sustained by any vision of transcendency nor revivified by individual genius. For principles they substitute recipes; for idiosyncrasies, tricks of the trade.

The practice of sculpture fortified Modigliani in the exercise of that freedom towards which, from the day he arrived in Paris until he met Brancusi, he had been slowly progessing.

The Servant Girl, 1915. Oil. ▷

66

67

Portrait of Jacques Lipchitz, 1917. Pencil.

I recall a scene, one night (it must have been in 1917) very late, maybe three o'clock in the morning.

We were suddenly aroused from our sleep by a terrific pounding on the door. I opened. It was Modigliani, obviously quite drunk. In a shaky voice he tried to tell me he remembered seeing on my shelf a volume of poetry by François Villon and he said he would like to have it. I lighted my kerosene lamp to find the book, hoping that he would leave so that I could go back to sleep. But no; he settled down in an armchair and began to recite in a loud voice.

I was living at that time at 54 rue de Montparnasse in a house occupied by working people, and soon my neighbors began to knock on the walls, on the ceiling, on the floor of my room, shouting, "Stop that noise!"

This scene is still vivid in my mind: the small room, the darkness of the middle of the night interrupted only by the flickering, mysterious light of the kerosene lamp, Modigliani, drunk, sitting like a phantom in the armchair, completely undisturbed, reciting Villon, his voice growing louder and louder, accompanied by an orchestra of knocking sounds from all around our little cell. Not until he exhausted himself, hours later, did he stop.

JACQUES LIPCHITZ (1954)

Jacques Lipchitz and His Wife, 1916. Oil. ▷

Modigliani and the "Modiglianis"

M ODIGLIANI's undeviating practice of a chosen manner of seeing—a sort of passionate conformity—and the fact that his brush and pencil tended automatically, one would almost say, to recur to the same accents again and again, might lead a superficial observer to see in his work a certain monotony or, as an art critic might prefer to style it, mannerism.

Yet even if we allow for the fact that the artist died just when he had reached the height of his powers, that the bulk of his production, and the best of it, was crowded into the decade 1910-1920, and that during this period his creative work was persistently interrupted and impeded by drinking bouts, by the inroads of disease, by the slow erosion of poverty; even if we sort out the masterpieces from the corpus of his paintings (whose abundance is amazing when we remember the brief span of his life), eliminating those less successful canvases in which the painter almost seems to be parodying his own style: even when we compare the straight, inflexible line of Modigliani's evolution with the labyrinthine complex of experiments, periods and manners associated with Picasso, or, to a less degree, Matisse—even then we do not come away from an attentive study of his art with that impression of sameness and monotony which a cursory inspection of it might produce.

What the public asks of a painter today, above all else, are pictures which, whether the painter's name is written on them or not, are *signed works*; in other words, paintings that are recognizable as his at a glance, whether or not their provenance is known; the type of work confronted by which even the least expert observer may confidently declare, at the

Self-Portrait, c. 1918.
Pencil on cream paper.

Raimondo, c. 1916. Oil.

Adrienne, 1917. Oil.

sole risk of being misled by a fake or copy: "Ah! That's a Modigliani!"

Yet when you stop and think about it, Modigliani painted fewer "Modiglianis" than it seems.

Now what exactly is a Modigliani of this truly distinctive type, a "Modigliani-Modigliani," as it might be called?

It is a portrait, most usually one of a woman, handled in the decorative portrait tradition of the Italian masters. The line meets the eye clearly at every point, clean-cut and firm. It animates the picture surface, organizing it throughout in a rhythm of sinuous curves, melodious and light as gossamer. It suggests the human body in all its plenitude by resorting to distortions which, while wholly arbitrary, are completely satisfying to the senses: neck and hands are inordinately—yet exquisitely—elongated; the torso as a rule is relatively short; the head, tiny in proportion to the body, is built up around the long straight line of the nose; the eyes are usually two almonds tinted light blue, grey or green, without any definite indication of the pupil. As a rule the model is seated on a chair in a graceful attitude of languid, dreamy melancholy, which we are free to interpret as *morbidezza* one hundred per cent

Crouching Nude, Turned Left, ▷
c. 1917. Pencil on wove paper.

72

73

Italian, as vegetative indifference one hundred per cent modern, or as the gentle afterglow of sensuality gratified. The sitter is almost invariably shown in front view. But it is in the layout, the *mise en page*, always flawlessly accomplished, that the artist displays his superb inventive skill, his unerring taste, the subtlety of his visual computations, his gift of creating all-pervasive rhythm with all-but-invisible arabesques.

Characteristic of the palette of the essential works—the "Modigliani-Modiglianis"—is the dominant note of an intensely warm and luminous flesh tint that makes the face, neck, arms and hands stand out against garments and background. It consists of orange, mixed with vermilion and two or three yellows, edged with a thin line of black or bistre.

Some of the artist's finest pictures are, in fact, these "Modigliani-Modiglianis." One of his loveliest nudes is *Elvira*, painted two years before he died and certainly the most popular of all his works. This painting may be taken as synthesizing all those characteristic traits which might be described as Modigliani's *manner*, were it not truer to describe them as his *style*. The seated figure tells out against a blue ground scumbled with grey, green and yellow-white. The girl is seen in front view, and the cool hue of the body bathed

Woman with a Collaret (Madame Zborowska), 1917. Oil. Detail of page 82. ▷

Elvira with a White Collar, 1918. Oil.

Elvira, 1918. Oil.

in glancing lights, with arms and neck elongated and modeled with a mellowness reminiscent of Renoir, is stressed by two dark accents, her jet-black hair and the dull black of the chair. She stands, or rather sits, slightly askew, to the left of center, a vertical band of deeper blue at the extreme right enlarging that side of the picture just enough to accentuate the impression of a delicately poised unbalance. Her hands are awkwardly—but how expertly!—placed on the white linen, whose texture is built up with low-toned greys, with greens and a dash of bistre and black, so as to bring out the rich glow of her body as it drinks in great draughts of light from the upper right—or is not the body itself aglow, lit by an inner radiance?

Seated Nude, 1917. Oil.

Nude (Elvira), 1918. Oil. ▷

76

Looking at this canvas, which brings to mind not only the European masters of the nude, from Cranach to Degas and Renoir, but also the great Hindu Apsaras of the tenth century and Benvenuto Cellini's *Nymph of Fontainebleau*, we are reminded of a sonnet by the great Italian poet whom Modigliani loved above all others:

> Love's color and the semblance of deep ruth
> Were never yet shown forth so perfectly
> In any lady's face, chancing to see
> Grief's miserable countenance uncouth,
> As in thine, lady...

But though in most of Modigliani's portraits of women we find that "piteous countenance" to which Dante alludes in the commentaries of his *Vita Nuova* ("... a pale color," he writes, "as though of love..."), the nudes are instinct with a sensuality for which it is not easy to find a parallel in art. The High Renaissance masters, Titian, Tintoretto, Giorgione, extolled the nude as a kind of crown jewel, majestic and radiant, set in the sublimated glory of a landscape designed—always a little theatrically—to enhance the sovereign opulence of the female body. With Rubens and Jordaens the nude has a Baroque luxuriance of fleshly charms, gloated over, often as not, by some monster of virility, lust incarnate. With the eighteenth-century painters nudity was provocative and gay. Rembrandt and Goya were almost alone in giving their nudes a poetic appeal, discreet yet potent, far removed from the

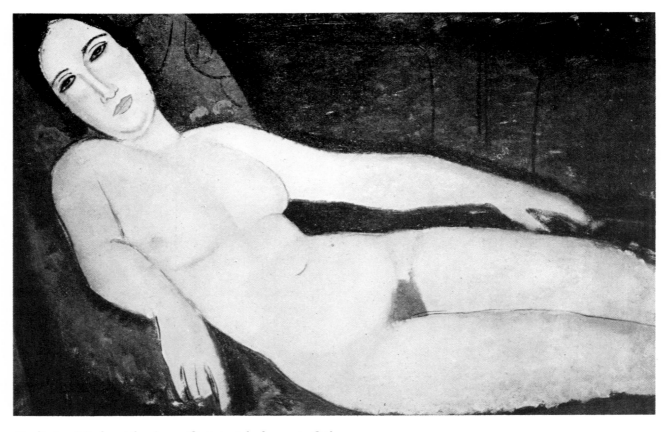

Reclining Nude with Arms Outstretched, 1916. Oil.

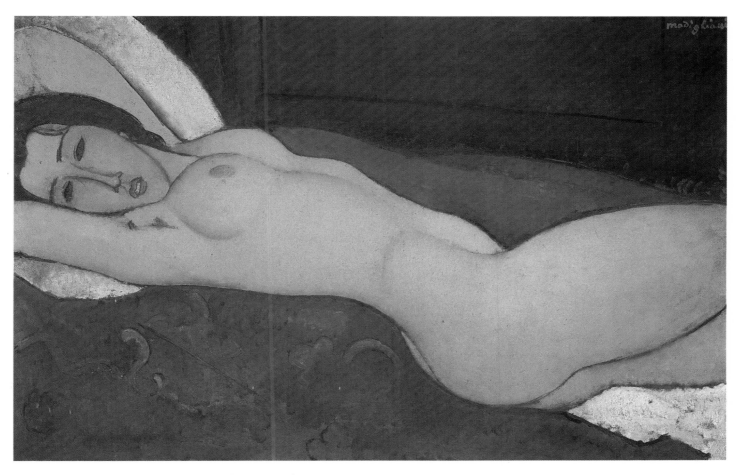

Reclining Nude with Hands Behind her Head, 1917. Oil.

ruling spirit of the painting of their time—Rembrandt's from the gross revelry of the Dutch kermis, Goya's from the elegant indecency of the eighteenth century. But when we analyse the smoldering sensuality of Modigliani, we are inevitably led to give him a place in the lineage of those Late Renaissance Italians who, long before his time, so greatly enriched the tradition of French painting: Niccolo dell'Abbate and Primaticcio.

And to these names must be added that of another great artist, one who, like Modigliani, was all for novel arabesques and languorous, swan-like elongations of women's necks: that master draftsman, Ingres.

What Baudelaire said of Ingres is also true, by and large, of Modigliani (anyhow of the Modigliani we are here concerned with): "He uses line in accordance with a system. He believes that nature should be corrected, amended; that a felicitous piece of trickery indulged in with a view to pleasing the eye, is not only the artist's right but his duty... Here, for example, is a cluster of fingers too uniformly elongated, unnaturally tapered. Carried away by an almost morbid preoccupation with style, the painter often dispenses with modeling altogether, or else reduces it almost to invisibility, intent as he is on giving more prominence to outlines."

When confronted by an artist who practises this "felicitous trickery," even the most lucid and open-minded observer is apt to be left, despite himself, with an uneasy feeling that natural forms are being profaned, for these are words that recur again and again in the writings of our critics. Even Baudelaire describes Ingres' preoccupation with style as "almost morbid," while Bernard Dorival declares that Modigliani's paintings give off "a pungent, unwholesome fragrance"—not to mention the pronouncements of Maurice Barrès on the "morbid emotivity" of El Greco, or the opinions of those censorious critics who detect "perversity" in Chagall and "vice" in Courbet. Nor was there any difficulty in 1918 in finding a police official who was ready to endorse these views on art (backed, as we have seen, by eminent authorities) and who, in the name of the law, had Modigliani's nudes removed from the show-window of Berthe Weill's gallery.

Seated Nude, Right Leg
Bent Under, c. 1917. Pencil.

Seated Nude, 1916. Oil. ▷

81

But if he makes the small effort of will that is needed to look at Modigliani's works with an unprejudiced eye, disregarding all the dubious legends that have grown up around them, it seems to me highly unlikely that anyone, however squeamish, will detect even the faintest trace of unwholesomeness, perversity or morbidity. In any case the criteria of moral and physical hygiene are usually inapplicable when we are dealing with works of art. Those prudish pedants who think they can test a picture for health and sanity remind me of the medical officers who take the height and weight of a conscript and without more ado pronounce him fit or unfit for armed service. What Modigliani expresses is often a mood of brooding, tranquil melancholy, sometimes gentle sensuality, never anything perverse or morbid.

Subjective and wholly personal as those derogatory opinions are, we may well suspect them of being often founded not so much on an appraisal of the works themselves as on circumstances having no direct bearing on them. There has been, for example, an attempt to ascribe their special qualities to the fact that Modigliani was of Jewish descent. One historian of modern art, who cannot for a moment be suspected of racial prejudice in any form and whose admiration for Modigliani is expressed in many pages of excellent criticism, concludes his study of the artist with a curious

Woman with a Collaret (Madame Zborowska), 1917. Oil.

Portrait of a Woman in a Green Blouse, 1917. Oil. ▷

Young Woman (Victoria), 1916. Oil. ▷▷

82

pronouncement. "Why," he asks, "is it that Modigliani's painting can no more be described as Italian art than Chagall's as Russian art? The reason is that Chagall and Modigliani are not only Russian and Italian respectively, but also Jewish, as are Pascin, Kisling and Soutine, and this accounts for the strain of exacerbated intellectualism and the deeply pessimistic view of life implicit in their art." The shallowness of these observations, with their rather astonishing parallels, is obvious. It is as pointless to discuss whether or not Modigliani's painting is Italian (or French, or Parisian) as it is to try to decide whether Picasso should be styled a Spanish painter or an artist of the School of Paris. The truth is, simply, that Modigliani was an Italian painter who lived in Paris where his art took shape in the international ferment of the Montmartre and Montparnasse of 1910, and as time went on it came more and more under the influence of the Sienese Primitives in particular and the Italians in general. It is hard to see what his art can possibly owe to his Jewish descent, and the parallel with Chagall and Pascin is far-fetched to say the least of it. Moreover, though Kisling and Soutine were close friends of Modigliani, his work is utterly different from theirs. Finally, who will deny that a very decided effort is required to read into his art either an "exacerbated intellectualism" or a "deeply pessimistic view of life"?

Intelligence of Modigliani

PERHAPS, after all, "intellectualism" is but a slightly invidious way of saying "intelligence"—when this latter is of a kind that leaves us feeling a little ill at ease. In Europe and America today, to say of a man that he is "highly intelligent" is to pay him a compliment. To say that he is "highly intellectual" often suggests one has misgivings about him. Now the case of Modigliani, as it happens, is one that might give rise to misgivings of this kind. The man was cultured, addicted to philosophy, well read in the poets; the artist was an inveterate museum-goer, and took a lively interest in all that was going on around him and the problems of the age. No question about it: he was an intellectual.

This much, however, is undeniable: whether or not it be "sensuous," "morbid," "tragic" or "decadent," Modigliani's painting is pre-eminently intelligent.

And it is just this intelligence of his that accounts for the rich diversity of his work. If Modigliani conforms less consistently than might be expected to our preconceived ideas of him, and if time and again he paints canvases that fail to correspond to the essential Modiglianis to which our eye has become accustomed, this is because his mind is alert, his intelligence always on the qui vive.

Intelligent comprehension of the model, first of all. Modigliani was able to bring a whole new world of poetry into being because everything he painted was the product of a never-failing sensibility. But it would be a very great mistake to believe that the haughty melancholy of Modigliani, the man, left its imprint on every face he painted and forced them all, in equal measure, to reflect his own temperament.

Portrait of Jean Cocteau, 1917, detail of page 87.

Portrait of Leopold Zborowski, 1916. Oil.   *Portrait of Leon Bakst, 1917. Oil.*

Great artists are much greater makers and leaders of nations than are monarchs and presidents. El Greco created a race of El Grecos; Renoir rules over an earthly paradise inhabited by countless Renoirs in the guise of children, girls and bathers; and Picasso, who in the sphere of painting holds imperial sway over a confederation comparable to that of the old Austro-Hungarian Empire, with a multitude of peoples and races subject to his authority—Picasso himself, whether creating the Harlequins of his Blue Period, the buxom matrons of his Neo-Classical Period or the nymphs and fauns of his summer-holiday interludes, presides over a nation of Picassos. But while Modigliani created for himself a principality whose citizens are all provided with a Modiglianian passport, the fact remains that only extremely careless observation or downright astigmatism can account for the notion that, because they have a family likeness, all his personages are substantially the same.

That instinctive understanding of human individuality which was one of Modigliani's gifts is interpreted in his portraits by variations of technique. At first sight of this or that

Portrait of Jean Cocteau, 1917. Oil.

picture, one is sometimes tempted to assign it to one or other of those periods of his career when he was, it seems, concerned particularly with exploring certain technical problems. Observe, for example, the angular design, the predilection for straight lines and geometric forms that characterize *Bride and Groom* (1915), the *Portrait of Beatrice Hastings* (1915), the *Portrait of Jean Cocteau* (1917); all this might be put down to the interest the artist was taking at the time in the experiments of his Cubist friends. Then, again, in other portraits, we might be inclined to read a predominant Tuscan influence into their underlying architecture of ovals and broadly flowing curves. But when we take the trouble to examine these pictures, we discover that the special nature of the drawing depends in every case on the personality of the model. Within the space of a few weeks Modigliani painted the portrait of Zborowski, that of Cocteau, and one of the earliest of his portraits of Jeanne Hébuterne. To speak for a moment in superficial, over-simplified terms, we might say that in the portrait of Zborowski the dominant geometric element is the circle, in the portrait of Cocteau the acute

Portrait of Hanka Zborowska, 1916. Oil.

Portrait of Max Jacob, 1916. Oil.

angle, in the portrait of Jeanne Hébuterne the oval. So as to convey at once the nimbleness and sparkle of Cocteau's wit and his elfin cast of face, Modigliani imparted to his line, and indeed to the whole composition, an angularity and a nervous restlessness at the opposite pole from his rendering of Zborowski's face, which with its mild-eyed meekness reminds us of a faithful sheepdog's. And when for the first time the face of Jeanne Hébuterne appears, the woman he must always have dreamed of, though (like Leopardi before him) he may have felt, as he sought her in the crowd, that she was *la donna che non si trova*, the woman one never meets—when she appears on the scene, then Modigliani's line acquires a delicate, melodious grace, and he employs a *forma semplificata a perdita di carezza*, "form simplified to the ghost of a caress," to use a phrase applied to Modigliani's drawings by the Italian critic Raffaello Franchi.

Though the dominant note in most of Modigliani's portraits seems to be one of melancholy and wistful loneliness, these are far from being the only sentiments or the only moods he is capable of expressing. The young models who seem so bored as they wait for the sitting to be over, lost perhaps in somber thoughts about the rent to be paid, the passing of their youth, the tediousness of their lives; the

Young Man in a Striped Sweater, ▷
1917. Oil.

90

Portrait of Chaïm Soutine, c. 1918. Pencil.

servant girls with their hands in their laps, worn out with
having made so many beds, with being nagged at and brow-
beaten, with daily backaches and an exhausting struggle to
make ends meet; the undernourished children, unloved and
uncared-for, whom the painter was perhaps the only one to
hold and cherish for a moment—Modigliani was capable of
portraying not only such as these, but also the complacent
and self-satisfied, the prosperous and successful, fortune's
favorites with money in the bank and a place in the sun. The
famous picture dealer Paul Guillaume—who was obviously
aware of the painter's talent since he bought many canvases
from him—is reported as having said to Zborowski, with
reference to Modigliani's art: "There's nothing French about
it, and that's a great pity because the young man has a real
gift." If he really made such a statement, then there is certainly some justification for reading into Modigliani's portraits of
Paul Guillaume a discreet retaliation on the artist's part. In
the 1915 portrait the head is slightly thrown back, the eyes
look out at us with a vacant, supercilious stare, and a cigarette
dangles loosely in the hand; everything suggests a self-
conceit which we find reiterated with the same involuntary

Portrait of Chaïm Soutine, ▷
1916. Oil.

93

94

Elena, 1917. Oil.

rancor in the 1916 portrait in Milan. And in one and the same year (1918) Modigliani was capable of painting that wonderful *Portrait of an Apprentice*—instinct with compassion for a boy exhausted by a hard day's work, his childish face resting on a large red hand, while the other hand drops listlessly upon his lap—and the scathing *Portrait of a Woman with a Cigarette*, a creature of pampered ease and smugness.

With Modigliani changes of technique never imply a quest of form for form's sake. Thus, in the case of the nudes, it is easy to differentiate the procedure followed in such a picture as the *Little Milkmaid* from that of the large *Reclining Nudes* in the Museum of Modern Art and the Mattioli Collection. To express the emotions aroused by the adolescent body of the young milkmaid, Modigliani resorted to a flickering, tenuous line and limpid, evenly diffused light. Between flesh tints and background (very pale scumblings of pink and green), instead of oppositions and contrasts, we find subtly modulated transitions. But in the large reclining nudes outlines are rendered with forcible directness and the brown backgrounds bring out the glowing ochre of the carnations. In short, the spirit of these two categories of nudes is completely different.

◁ *Portrait of Oscar Miestchaninoff, 1916. Oil.*

95

When we are told that Modigliani's nudes are sensual, or that they are erotic, we are in fact told nothing at all about them; the deeper issues are ignored. Obviously the sensuality emanating from the *Little Milkmaid* is not in the same vein as that which infuses the large reclining nudes—just as the atmosphere evoked by *Daphnis and Chloe* is quite other than that evoked in *La Fille aux yeux d'or* or Baudelaire's *Les Bijoux*. I have touched on the marked differences of the color schemes and linear patterns in these pictures; crisp and emphatic in some, merely hinted at in others. Even the layout and format vary considerably, and always for well-founded reasons. In the *Little Milkmaid* and the *Portrait of Jeanne Hébuterne* in the Metropolitan Museum, the model is shown three-quarter length and in both canvases we find a curious ambivalence, sensuality at odds with modesty, passion with decorum, desire with a shrinking from desire. In these works the female body has something of the quality of those early morning landscapes that emerge from mist at daybreak. On the other hand, owing both to the horizontal format and their compositional rhythms, the reclining nudes produce a very different impression, one of shameless abandon, of ardent, untrammelled passion. These might be described as "night pieces," whereas the others are "morning pieces."

Portrait of Paul Guillaume ▷
"Novo Pilota", 1915. Oil.

Portrait of Paul Guillaume, 1916. Pencil.

Portrait of Paul Guillaume, 1916. Oil.

98

Lucienne, 1916. Oil.

The Servant Girl, 1916. Oil.

*◁ Madame Amédée
(Woman with Cigarette),
1918. Oil.*

For further illustrations of Modigliani's versatility, of his psychological insight as a portrait painter and the adroitness with which he adapted his technique to the temperament of the model before him, we need only compare the two portraits of Soutine with those of Max Jacob or with the earlier portraits of Diego Rivera. In each case Modigliani renewed his palette and created an appropriate style. The four Soutine portraits not only record the features of his friend, but also constitute a sort of Homage to Soutine. They are loaded with those violent colors which recur so often in Soutine's own paintings. They are at once typically Modiglianesque and profoundly Soutinesque; it is almost as if Modigliani, in the course of the work, had combined discreet pastiche with a psychological study of his artist friend. On the other hand, in the portraits of Max Jacob and Diego Rivera he employed a quite different range of technical means, ingeniously adapted to the personalities of his sitters.

One day André Masson let fall the ironical remark that, were Cézanne alive today, he would be advised to name the portrait of his wife *Portrait of Madame Cézanne's Dress*. Had any such suggestion been made to Modigliani, he would certainly have turned it down indignantly. True, the surface

Nude on a Blue Cushion, 1917. Oil.

*Seated Nude
(La Belle Romaine), 1917,
detail of page 104.*

qualities of his canvases consist of a certain number of favorite recipes and reveal a preference for certain colors and linear rhythms, but overriding all else, in everything he did, was a passionate interest in the human individual, in the mystery and meaning of a personality. He was not content simply to create a pattern of "colors assembled in a certain order"; he created living beings, with the order or disorder that comes of individual temperaments inscribed on their faces.

But once again the Modigliani legend intervenes between his pictures and our response to them. It is somewhat exasperating when an art critic who, as a matter of fact, admires Modigliani, sees in his Jewish origin the *key* to his work. And then we have that other critic who, after an intelligent appreciation of the concision, restraint and elegance of Modigliani's art, in which he finds indications of a quite amazing culture, touched with genius, professes to detect in the faces of his figures, "not the mystery and spirituality of Fra Angelico" but "a kind of stupor induced by drugs." The chances are that, had this critic known nothing of that dark side of Modigliani's life (which he resolutely excluded from his art), it

Reclining Nude, c. 1917. Oil.

would never have occurred to him to interpret that poignant silence we can sense in certain portraits as a result of drug-taking. For is there really any need to invoke the artificial paradise of the drug-addict as an explanation of that curious torpor weighing down the children and young working-class women portrayed by Modigliani? Surely the hard realities of daily life are quite enough to impose on faces a look of stolid indifference, due not to drugs but to poverty; a look which has nothing to do with an escape from reality, but is the outcome of hardship and privations, of that joyless life so

Reclining Nude, c. 1919. Oil.

Reclining Nude, detail of page 79. ▷

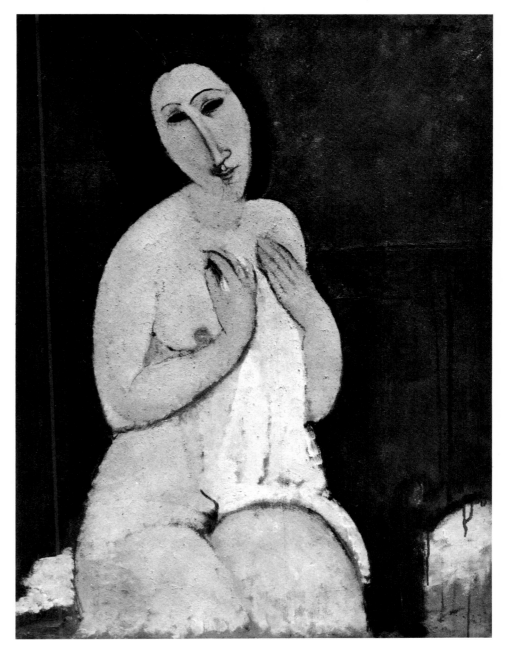

Seated Nude with a Chemise, 1917. Oil.

Seated Nude
(La Belle Romaine),
1917. Oil.

well described—before all too soon he succumbed to it—by another great Italian, Cesare Pavese. Not that Modigliani ever indulged in picturesque portrayals of the seamy side of life for their own sake, though he could hardly have been blamed for doing so. There is, rather, in that sense of latent joy which shines out even in his most harrowing canvases, something that reminds us of a saying of Pavese: "Life holds but a single pleasure, that of being alive; all the rest is sorrow." And Modigliani never ceased to gaze with wondering, enraptured eyes at Life—that wonderful, absurd adventure which slowly but surely wears us out, day after day, until our last.

The Business of Living

SOON after coming to Paris, Modigliani jokingly remarked that he'd only found a single buyer, and that was a blind man. André Warnod remembers this first Modigliani collector. It was an old man named Léon Angeli who lived in the Rue Gabrielle and, though not completely, was very nearly blind. Angeli made a practice of buying canvases from the younger generation of painters, on the theory that, by the law of averages, he was bound to strike a winner now and then. Hard hit by the war, Angeli sold his entire stock of pictures, winners and losers indiscriminately, for a song. He died in abject poverty in 1921.

Modigliani's meeting with Dr Paul Alexandre in 1908 brought him the solace of friendship with a man who not only admired and believed in his work, but gave him material encouragement by making regular purchases. Dr Alexandre was far from being rich, but over a period of years he spent a considerable part of his income on building up the Modigliani collection which he jealously kept intact until his death.

It would seem that, during Modigliani's lifetime, neither picture dealers nor professional critics appraised his work at its true value. As a man he attracted attention by the Bohemian life he led, tempestuous and colorful to a degree; as an artist, on the other hand, he often gave an impression of being unduly timid, even academic in his painting.

In the Paris of that time, when an almost frenzied quest of novelty—of originality at all costs—was the order of the day, his persistent efforts to restore the links with the oldest traditions of painting and to retrace the "Ariadne's clew" of the Byzantine, Sienese and Gothic styles, seemed pathetically outmoded.

There can be little question that in everyday life Modigliani was not easy to get on with, nor a restful companion. He could be altogether charming, even fascinating, winning friends easily "with the melodious warmth of his voice and the aura of poetry that emanated from his whole person." But all too often, especially after drinking, excitement got the better of his saner self and his conversation took a truculent, aggressive turn.

All who knew him have paid tribute to his generosity and courage. Louis Latourrettes tells how, one evening in a café at Montmartre, Modigliani challenged a group of rowdies who were loudly airing their anti-Semitic views, by walking straight up to their table and telling them to their faces: "I'm a Jew and you can all go to hell!" It was characteristic of Modigliani to let himself go, recklessly, sometimes tactlessly, wherever he chanced to be. Thus on one occasion he burst into Jacques Lipchitz's room in the small hours of the morning, took up a volume of poetry by François Villon and started reciting at the top of his voice those marvelous ballads descriptive of a tragic destiny not unlike his own, while the neighbors, roused from sleep and not unreasonably indignant, hammered on the walls and yelled to him to stop. But Modigliani was in one of his moods of exaltation, aflame with wine and poetry, and nothing would induce him to desist.

Two Little Girls, 1918. Oil. ▷

Little Girl with a Black Apron, 1918. Oil.

Little Girl in Blue, 1918. Oil.

◁ Woman with Red Hair, 1917. Oil.

The Servant Girl (Marie Ferret), 1918. Oil.

The Black Dress, 1918. Oil.

Still, these were relatively mild indiscretions compared with the almost crazy fits of rage that came over him when he was under the influence of alcohol and hashish.

One effect of drink and drugs is that they bring up into the light what normally lies hidden in the dark underworld of consciousness. Fernande Olivier tells the story of an evening spent with Princet when he and his friends Max Jacob, Apollinaire and Picasso all took hashish. Each revealed his secret self with total unconstraint. Princet who had just lost his wife started weeping; Apollinaire imagined he was in a bawdyhouse and, while Max Jacob kept silent, Picasso fell to shouting that he had "discovered photography" and might as well kill himself, as he had nothing left to learn.

Under the influence of the drug something beneath the threshold of Picasso's consciousness had risen to the surface: that ambivalent obsession of his young days—the simultaneous fascination and repulsion photography had for him; that dream of creating a perfectly faithful image of the visible world and the fear that once this was done, there would be nothing left for him but to kill himself.

The effect of drink or drugs on Modigliani was a blind surrender to an urge for self-assertion. This indeed was

Marie (La Petite Marie), 1918. Oil.

◁ *Gypsy Woman with Baby, 1919. Oil.*

Little Girl with a Beret, 1918. Oil.

natural enough; he had worked so hard for recognition, but all to no avail. And there welled up a flood of memories and emotions: the hardships of his childhood, the struggles of his family to keep afloat, his pride in being a Jew, his anger at being poor. Drink had the effect of bringing out all his rankling grievances with life; gentlest of mortals in his sober hours, he became quarrelsome, obstreperous in his cups.

The outbreak of war made things even harder for him, materially speaking. Many of his friends, Dr Alexandre to begin with, were called up, and there was a general exodus from Paris. Relations with his family and the help he was getting from them became more and more precarious. We are told that Modigliani thought seriously of enlisting as a volunteer. Actually he saw the war through in Paris as a civilian; whether out of deference to the socialist pacifism of his brother, Giuseppe Emanuele, or because he was found unfit for service, there is no knowing.

This much, however, is known: that the war years were the blackest of Modigliani's life. Beatrice Hastings, a young English poetess, his devoted companion for nearly two years, was no less amazed by his industry than dismayed by her inability to check his wild excesses. He made several portraits of her, but his production in the first year of the war was meager.

From 1915 onward, however, Modigliani's output showed a steady rise; though his circumstances were becoming ever more straitened, it was now that his talent blossomed forth at its splendid best. This was undoubtedly due to the good offices of the obscure Polish exile whose acquaintance he made at the end of 1914 or the beginning of 1915: Leopold Zborowski.

It was Zadkine who introduced Amedeo to the young English poetess who bore the name of Dante's lady-love. And it was Kisling who arranged for him to meet Zborowski, a Polish poet who had set up as a picture dealer in a very small way in the Rue Joseph Bara. Zadkine has given a description of Modigliani's appearance at this time. "His chin, whose beauty we so much admired, was often masked by a shaggy, unkempt beard and his face was already furrowed by the ravages of hashish and heavy drinking." It is perhaps too flattering to describe Zborowski ("Zbo" for short) as a picture dealer; he was more of a picture peddler, with a fine enthusiasm for his wares. The connection between Modigliani and Zborowski, Lipchitz tells us, was "a remarkable instance of the close relationship, almost like a family tie, that existed between many artists and their dealers in the Paris of those days. And not all the latter were exploiters or slave drivers."

The Young Apprentice, 1918. Oil.

The Little Peasant, 1918. Oil.

Portrait of Leopold Zborowski, c. 1917.
Ink on lined paper.

"Modi" had already met several specimens of the slave-driving class. But in "Zbo" he found a man who was at once an impresario, a companion, an accomplice—and a loyal friend. While the painter worked, Zborowski hawked his canvases around Paris, doing his best to melt the hearts of the real picture dealers, the big men, and persuade them to buy the works of the unknown young Italian. Usually in vain. "Zbo used to come back in the evening," André Salmon tells us, "thoroughly worn out and on the brink of tears." Then to cheer themselves up they went off to dinner at Chez Rosalie, a restaurant in the Rue Campagne-Première, where the painter paid for his meals with a few drawings. Zadkine, that admirable sculptor who, had he elected for the pen rather than the chisel, might have been an excellent Russian novelist, devotes some realistic pages—which read like a tavern scene by Gorki—to a description of Modigliani at Chez Rosalie, where big rats, tired of nibbling the sketches

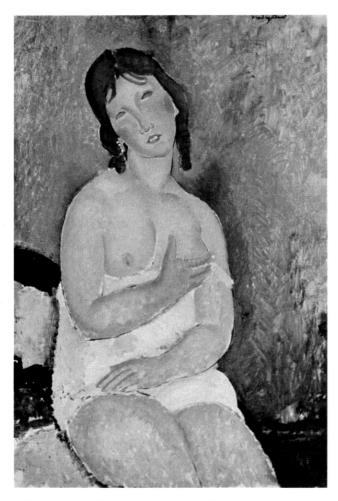

The Little Milkmaid, 1918. Oil.

Sitting Nude, c. 1917. Pencil.

that Rosalie, for want of anywhere to store them, flung light-heartedly into the cellar, "used to sneak up into the tiny kitchen, with bits of the drawings still in their mouths." If the story of the rats with shreds of drawings in their mouths may seem a little too far-fetched to be convincing, the atmosphere Zadkine conjures up is borne out by an incident evoked in Vlaminck's Memoirs. "One winter morning in 1917 I saw Modigliani standing on a street island in the Boulevard Raspail. With the haughty air of a general in charge of army manœuvres, he was watching the taxis streaming past. An icy wind was blowing, but the moment Modi saw me he came up and said, quite casually, as if referring to something he didn't need in the least: 'Look here, I'll sell you my overcoat, it's much too big for me and should fit you nicely.' "

It was about this time that one morning his compatriot Ubaldo Oppi, who then was living in the Place Emile-Goudeau, heard a ring at his bell, got up and opened the door. There stood Modigliani, carrying a suitcase.

"Oppi," he said, "I want you to buy this case."

"But I don't need a suitcase."

"I only want ten francs for it."

"Sorry, I'm on the rocks myself. That's why I'm staying in bed today, I haven't even got the price of a meal."

La Belle Epicière, 1918. Oil. ▷

Portrait of Lunia Czechowska, 1919. Oil.

"I was in the doorway," Oppi writes, "in my nightshirt, my legs bare. Modi had just put down the suitcase—an old canvas contraption with reinforced corners—and was standing there with dangling arms. We exchanged wry smiles. Then Modigliani shut his big, lustrous eyes, let his handsome head droop and bending down, picked up the suitcase.

" 'In that case...' he sighed."

But it was not quite the hackneyed story of the talented painter persistently cold-shouldered by dealers and public. In point of fact Zborowski's efforts had gradually borne fruit and even in the pre-war years some collectors were beginning to show an interest in Modigliani's work. True, for some time after the outbreak of war (as was only to be expected) the market for pictures dried up almost completely and the growth of Modigliani's reputation was inevitably retarded. All the same, slowly but surely he was making a name for himself. Though the nudes exhibited in the window of Berthe Weill's gallery in 1918 had to be removed on the ground of their indecency, this one-man show was a real success, not merely a *succès d'estime*. But Modigliani was nothing if not a spendthrift; no sooner did money touch his hands than it melted away like snow in sunlight. Zborowski compared him to "the vine which yields its grapes and asks for nothing in return." When Louis Latourrettes met Modigliani not long before his death the painter told him with an ironic twinkle in his eye: "I'm doing well financially nowadays. I'll soon be able to make investments. As you're a businessman you might tell me the name of a good stockbroker; considering my father's in the same line, he'll feel bound to give me some good tips." But the remark was not meant to be taken seriously; Modigliani was the last man in the world to make investments or to profit by "good tips."

It was in 1917 that, at that hub of chance encounters, the Café de la Rotonde in Montparnasse, destiny confronted Modigliani with the girl who was to be his loyal companion till death, and after death: Jeanne Hébuterne.

A Working Girl, 1919. Oil. ▷

Portrait of Jeanne Hébuterne, 1919. Oil. ▷▷

123

Vita Nuova

*When first the glorious Lady of my thoughts was
made manifest to mine eyes... at that moment, I say most
truly that the spirit of life, which hath its dwelling in the
secretest chamber of the heart, began to tremble so violently
that the least pulses of my body shook therewith.*

DANTE, LA VITA NUOVA
(adapted from Rossetti's translation)

THE concierge and neighbors used to say: "Isn't it just too
bad seeing a nice young man like that getting into such
dreadful states!"

For there was no denying, Monsieur Modigliani when he
wasn't "under the influence" was a real gentleman, with the
best of good manners and always the right thing to say, for-
eigner though he was.

Of course that cantankerous old fogy next door was
always grumbling about "those damned foreigners" who
spent their days and nights making a nuisance of themselves,
and never did a stroke of honest work. They'd have done
better to stay in their own countries and leave France to the
French—who anyhow had a right to be here, though by the
look of things you'd often think they hadn't.

But nobody listened to the old fellow, who soon gave it
up and buried his face in his newspaper, the *Echo de Paris*.

Vlaminck used to tell how he'd seen Modigliani at a table
in the Rotonde, dashing off sketches at lightning speed and
passing them on to the people at the other tables, with a lordly
gesture, like a millionaire handing out banknotes to a mob of
sycophants.

*Portrait of Jeanne Hébuterne,
detail of page 142.*

And the coal merchant often said things couldn't go on like that any longer, he'd have to cut off supplies.

But he went on giving credit because "Monsieur Modi had such a nice smile, such a way with him, you simply couldn't say No to him."

Then there was that Very Eminent Art Critic who said that all these undesirable aliens and Jews with faces like nothing on earth and accents you could cut with a knife were sapping the vitals of French art, soiling everything they touched.

They'd no business to be here, in the land of Jean Fouquet and Camille Corot and Maurice Denis.

And it was up to all good Frenchmen to keep their de-

Portrait of Jeanne Hébuterne in a Chemise, 1918. Oil.

generate, drink-sodden hands from tampering with the pure, gemlike flame of French tradition.

However, the American Lady to whom Modigliani presented an unsigned drawing one day at a café table, asked him —perhaps with a shrewd eye to the future—to be kind enough to sign it.

So he took a pencil and wrote his name in big block letters like the TO RENT notices in apartment windows.

Then by way of thanks she probably gave him motherly advice, told him he really shouldn't drink so much, he was playing fast and loose with his health, and so forth.

Foujita says that at this time Modigliani always wore corduroy suits, check shirts and a red belt:

that he was always drinking absinthe, the terrific Pernod of the past, and reciting poems.

And when people kept harping on the dangers of drink, he'd chuckle in a broad Italian accent, "I don't care!"

Zadkine tells us that his friend looked like a young god masquerading as a workman in his Sunday best.

Ramon Gomez de la Serna remembered quite well one night in the bar at the Rotonde,

Portrait of Jeanne Hébuterne, 1919. Oil.

when Mexican Diego Rivera and Amedeo started hurling insults at each other, surrounded by a ring of taxi drivers and ladies of the demi-monde.

Amedeo was shouting "Landscape! It simply doesn't exist!"

But Diego bawled him down. "Landscape *does* exist!"

Both are dead—at thirty-seven years' interval—and, likely as not, that night both of them were right.

"Still it's really sad to see so gifted a man as Modi drinking himself to death like that."

But the people who said this, with the best will in the world, failed to see

that though most of us want to go on living, some think life's not such a blessing after all and it's better "not to be."

Death for them is the line of least resistance

and they've no wish to prolong unduly their earthly existence.

One day Modigliani insulted Derain at a table in the Café Baty and made a scene.

Portrait of Jeanne Hébuterne, Arm Resting on a Chair, 1918. Oil.

He was a nice young man, but not always as polite as he might have been.

And if someone told him "That's not the way to behave, Modi,"

he'd answer, "Tell us another!" and finish off his drink.

As he was always coughing and spitting and looked so ill, Zborowski arranged with Leopold Survage to take him to Cagnes on the Riviera.

The story goes that his friends persuaded him to visit Renoir, then a very old man and half paralysed, but who went on painting with his brush strapped to his hand.

Old Renoir told the young Italian that he should paint "with love" and that personally he (Renoir) would spend whole days "stroking the backside of pretty girls" (with his brush, of course!).

And Modi, who had perhaps been drinking, answered rather rudely: "Personally, Mr Renoir, I've no use for rumps."

But of course he hadn't really caught the point that Renoir was trying to make clear

and in any case for both, oldster and youngster, the end was very near.

Zborowski remembered Modigliani's saying to him:

"I am leaving the mud behind, I now know all there is to know and soon I'll be no more than a handful of dust."

That was near the end, when he was like a sun that's run its course and is setting in the west.

But there was a girl he loved whose name was Jeanne, Jeanne Hébuterne, and with her he roamed the streets of Paris.

Hand in hand they often walked from the Lion of Belfort in Montparnasse to the Observatory,

each on one side of the ideal meridian line of Paris which, as it so happens, runs along the sidewalk of that street,

but it would be indiscreet

to speculate about what they said on those occasions; that was their own affair.

And now they both are dead, but Jeanne still looks out at us from those portraits whose tranquil air

comes as a surprise when we remember that Modigliani, according to the doctors, was gravely ill,

but went on drinking heavily and flared into a rage whenever he'd had a glass too many, as drinkers will.

But he was never in a rage when he stood before his canvas and gave the portraits of his "very gentle lady" all the loving, clear-eyed attention of which he was capable,

and we can be sure that Jeanne loved him, too, because Amedeo with all his faults was lovable.

As for the rest, the private life of Modi and his little friend, Mademoiselle Jeanne Hébuterne, all that, as we said before, was their own affair.

Nothing matters today but those immortal portraits: that gently drooping head and flowerlike face whose outline Jeanne's lover traced ever and again, unfaltering, with loving care.

◁ *Portrait of Jeanne Hébuterne, 1919. Oil.*

Portrait of Jeanne Hébuterne with Yellow Sweater, 1918-1919. Oil.

131

Her image, that was with me always, was an exultation of Love to subdue me.

DANTE, LA VITA NUOVA

N O ONE has ever met a girl in the street who really looked like the Jeanne Hébuterne we see in the twenty canvases on which Modigliani has immortalized her face. Levelheaded people when they read the rhapsodies of poets, when they listen to the foolish words of endearment lovers have coined for their private use, when they look at pictures or listen to strange music—when, in short, they come on anything that seems far-fetched—are inclined to ask themselves, "Now where on earth can that idea have come from?"

"Where on earth...?" That is a question which often rises to our lips when we look at Modigliani's portraits. For he must have got his ideas from *somewhere*, though, quite obviously, not from visual experience. He cannot have actually had before him as he stood at his easel this slim, strange young person, long-drawn as a cloudless, happy summer day. Let us imagine what the sensible people we have mentioned would make of her as she figures in the many portraits scattered about the world—not to mention the hundreds of drawings. Well, this girl whom Modigliani painted for the first time with a hat on (one of those cloche hats which were already being worn in 1917), and almost always after that bareheaded, in a beige sweater with a rolled neck, or a black bodice, or a white shirtwaist—well, it's certain that our sage observer would decide that, if she was like that in real life, with a head that long, she must have been a real sight! And then that neck of hers, which certainly has five vertebrae too

Portrait of Jeanne Hébuterne, 1919. Oil.

133

à Dermée
Modigliani

House at Cagnes, 1919. Oil.

136

many (see any textbook of anatomy), and her hands like no hands on earth! "That young woman," he would say, "is *disproportioned*, a freak of nature."

But this would only prove that our common-sense critic was ignorant of the demonstrable fact that in great loves and great styles disproportion is the rule.

From that night forth, the natural functions of my body began to be vexed and impeded, for I was given up wholly to thinking of this most gracious creature.

DANTE, LA VITA NUOVA

The first reaction of the sense that professes to be common sense, when confronted by the extravagances of a lyrical poem or the plastic extra-visions of a picture, is to laugh them out of court. Similarly the reaction of an observer who thinks himself impartial ("cold-blooded" would be truer) towards the follies of a lover whom another human creature can transport into a world of strange enchantments; whose whole being has been changed by the mere existence of that loved one—the natural reaction of our detached observer is to think: "She (or he) is nice enough, but I can't for the life of me see what he (or she) finds in her (or him)."

Manifestations of passion are always *disproportionate* to the object that arouses them. And nowhere in Modigliani's œuvre is this substitution of emotive for anatomical proportion so clearly demonstrated as in the twenty portraits celebrating the beauty of Jeanne Hébuterne.

In none of them do we find those carefully composed colors which characterize the portraits we have called the Modigliani-Modiglianis. That delightful, artificial flesh tint shot with glints of gold or coppery red, which imparts to his other nudes their plangent glow, is absent here. In most pictures of Jeanne we find a very discreet, deliberately subdued color orchestration. In the portrait which shows her lightly resting her left hand on her shoulder, the sole purpose of the contrast between the deep black of the blouse and the warm red of the skirt is to bring out the sinuous movement of the slim, pale arms. The chestnut hair, the pale ochre of Jeanne's face and neck, the light green and ochreous pinks of the background, all are pitched in a studiously lowered key. Similarly, in the two portraits where she is wearing a thick

The Notary from Nice, 1919. Oil.

Portrait of Hanka Zborowska with Clasped Hands, 1919. Oil.

brownish-yellow sweater with a rolled collar, the pictorial values are based on the relation between the chestnut hair and the unusual color of the sweater. Though in the portrait showing her with her shoulders wrapped in a red shawl, Modigliani plays the virtuoso in a set of variations in the key of red (there are no less than five distinct shades of red in the picture), here, too, his object is to emphasize the pale pure hues of the hair, neck and hands, rendered almost in monochrome. In another portrait we find him ringing the changes on various tones of black; the effect of the black dress and horizontal black band beside a band of yellow in the background is to accentuate the diffused radiance of the slanting oval of the face, and of the equally long neck, prolonged by the opening of the blouse; while the half-bare arms are relieved against the blackness of the skirt.

Scanning these love letters—for such they are—writ large on canvas, we realize how arbitrary is any attempt to appraise a work of art in terms of its moral qualities and to assign psychological values to the painter's choice of colors and their arrangement on the picture surface. Still in the present case this is perhaps excusable. For in the softness of the colors, the fragile delicacy of the tones and the exquisite discretion with which relationships between the picture elements are stated, we cannot fail to sense the expression of a love no less discreet than ecstatic. Modigliani is speaking here almost in a whisper; he *murmurs* his painting as a lover murmurs endearments in the ear of his beloved. And the light bathing this picture is the light of adoration.

What our young prince errant of the streets of Montparnasse who at this very time was playing havoc with the brief span of life remaining to him, has bodied forth in these portraits is that enchanted silence which binds us with its spell when we contemplate these works in which a man who was a misfit in the scheme of things drew from the fragile presence of a woman the strength to hope anew: the silence of the Buddhist statues of Kwan Yin, Goddess of Pity; of the icons in which an adoring Russian painter celebrates Our Lady of Compassions; of Simone Martini's *Annunciation* in the Uffizi, where the Virgin shrinks away, dumbfounded by the angel's message.

Modigliani had lived wildly, laughing, quarreling and brawling; had "scattered roses riotously with the throng."

The Flower Vendor, 1919. Oil.

Portrait of Lunia Czechowska, 1919. Oil.

139

The Swedish Girl, 1919. Oil.

Portrait of Lunia Czechowska, 1918. Oil.

Head of a Woman, c. 1918. Oil.

Portrait of Thora Klinckowström, 1919. Oil.

Portrait of Jeanne Hébuterne, 1918. Oil.

Man with a Hat (Portrait of Mario the Musician), 1920. Pencil.

Now that the tumult and the shouting has died away, all to reach our ears is echoes, faintly transmitted by those who chanced to meet him in those far-off years.

André Salmon tells of the last occasion when he saw the two young lovers. Amedeo was in a furious temper with Jeanne. "He was dragging her along by an arm, gripping her frail wrist, tugging at one or other of her two long braids of hair, and only letting go of her a moment to send her crashing against the iron railings of the Luxembourg. He was like a madman, crazy with rage, with savage hatred."

All that is ended; the better part remains: love's silence, that silence of which Dante spoke and which Modigliani has enshrined in his art.

> *Tanto gentile e tanto onesta pare*
> *La donna mia quand'ella altrui saluta,*
> *Ch'ogne lingua deven tremando muta,*
> *E li occhi no l'ardiscon di guardare.*

> My lady looks so gentle and so pure
> When yielding salutation by the way,
> That the tongue trembles and has nought to say,
> And the eyes, which fain would see, may not endure.

Portrait of Mario Varvogli, ▷
1919. Oil.

143

Reclining Nude, the Right Arm under her Head, 1919. Oil.

144

Cruel Death, Pity's Foe

Morte villana, di pietà nemica,
Di dolor madre antica,
Giudicio incontastabile gravoso...

Cruel death, pity's foe,
ancient mother of grief,
merciless judgment without appeal...

DANTE, LA VITA NUOVA

ON November 29, 1918, a daughter was born to Modigliani and Jeanne Hébuterne: Jeannette, "Nannoli."

One night in January 1920, when Modi was walking with some friends from the Rue de la Tombe-Issoire to Denfert-Rochereau, he waited in the street while the others escorted one of the party to a room on the top floor. He remained for several minutes seated on one of the benches on the sidewalk, shaking with cold and cursing his friends for their desertion.

Next morning he was running a high temperature, with shivering fits, and had to be taken, much against his will, to the Hôpital de la Charité.

His friend Ortiz de Sarate told André Salmon that a few days before this Amedeo had said to him: "You know, I've only a tiny bit of brain left. I can't help feeling it's the end."

When leaving for the hospital he said (so Florent Fels recounts) to the same friend: "I've kissed my wife. Please take her back to her parents, this is the right moment. Anyhow, we're sure of eternal happiness, she and I, whatever happens."

On January 25, 1920, he died in hospital. It is said that his last whispered words were: *"Cara, cara Italia."*

When she heard of his death, Jeanne Hébuterne, who was expecting another child, flung herself from a window of her parents' fifth-floor apartment.

His brother wired from Rome: "Bury him like a prince."

And—the rest is silence.

Motherhood, 1919. Pencil.

Life is a Gift

ART historians, and critics in particular, have a predilection for tracing links between the artists they discuss and their contemporaries. This is impossible in Modigliani's case. Though in his art and in his life he formed some deep attachments, he never belonged to any school or was anyone's disciple. Like Kipling's "Cat Who Walked by Himself," he went his own way. Although he may have produced the impression of a boon companion and an extrovert when drinking the night away in the company of friends, in fact he unbosomed himself to nobody—except in his painting. But what he lets us see of himself in his painting is the *essential* Modigliani.

Yet this man of genius whose art contained so little of the anecdotal was the predestined prey of anecdote-mongers; this secret prince has been time and again a victim of obtuse contemporaries who have thought fit to weave around his life a questionable legend rather than to appraise his unquestionable genius. Thus, though his career as an artist was a victorious progress from strength to strength, he is often represented as the pathetic hero of a twentieth-century *Vie de Bohème*. Of all those who were in touch with Modigliani, I prefer to listen to that loyal friend who first perceived his real greatness. "It doesn't do to believe all the tales you've heard about him," Dr Alexandre told me. "What struck me most about Amedeo was that he was such a well-bred man." *Un homme très bien élevé.* Perhaps he had also in mind the other meaning of the word "élevé"; a man "uplifted," who aimed high and scaled the heights. A writer who knew him much later, near the end of his life, confirmed this opinion. "I remember him as a courteous, reserved man," Charles-Albert

Cingria said. "No doubt he drank too much and sometimes got a bit uproarious, but no more so than other young men of the day. What struck one was the *quality* of that uproariousness; however excited, he always remained a gentleman." It is pleasant to have Cingria's eyewitness testimony that the too common conception of Modigliani as a vulgar brawler or an exhibitionist mountebank acting the part of the "outcast painter," bugbear of the bourgeois, is a fallacy.

The ideas behind his art may well have struck many of his contemporaries as out of date, reactionary. The influence of Cézanne—whom he studied attentively—was paramount at the time, and, like the Aix master, most vanguard artists were trying to render perspective by means of color alone; while others attacked the object, mangled and disintegrated it, making it explode in a space-dimension scared, one would say, out of existence. There was perhaps only one other painter of the day equally obsessed with drawing, and that was Picasso. As Hokusai was known as the "old man mad on drawing," so Modigliani might be called the pencil-crazy draftsman. Carried off by death at an early age—like Masaccio, Giorgione, Watteau and Géricault—he left behind him thousands of pencil drawings. If some cataclysm had deprived the world of all Modigliani's paintings and spared the drawings, the latter would certainly have assured him a front-rank place as a superb interpreter of human bodies and faces, midway between Matisse and Picasso. Modigliani's drawings, portraits and nudes, all alike give that impression which is basic to the enjoyment of great works of art: a sense of fine economy. For in the last analysis all the qualities we most admire—elegance, concision, suggestive power and penetrating insight—sum up to this. Modigliani is one of the supremely gifted few who seem to say everything with next to nothing; in whose works a simple line, a brief allusion, a faintly indicated gesture suffice to bring before us all the infinite, incredible profusion of human life.

Modigliani's career as an artist was one long meditation on the mystery of the human face. His masterpieces inspire the same respect and awe that we feel when, gazing up at the vault of the Torcello basilica, we see the Virgin and Child floating in a sea of golden light; or when we contemplate the Virgins in the paintings of the Sienese masters. Modigliani transposed the celestial vision of the great painters he revered and loved on to the mundane plane of the easel picture, and erected a private Byzantium in the heart of a cosmopolitan Babel. He was an uncrowned Basileus of the private life of the world beyond the world, a Fra Amedeo of the fallen angels. Gifted though he was with a flair for selecting from very different sources—from the early Sienese to the recently discovered African art—whatever served his turn, Modigliani harked back continually, without the least trace of pastiche or conscious reminiscence, to that pure tradition of the apotheosis of the human visage which was transmitted from

Motherhood, 1919. Oil.

Byzantium to the Sienese, from Lorenzetti to Botticelli. In early youth Modigliani described beauty as "a fruit of the noblest strivings of the soul" and he kept faith with this dictum throughout his brief career. In that amazing sublimation of the visible which we find in his best works we can sense these noble strivings of the soul. In them we find deep feeling without a trace of sentimentality, emotive power without rhetorical exaggeration, tenderness without any taint of mawkishness, intense expression without expressionism.

Those who kept him company in his leisure hours, when the strain of pure creation was relaxed; who drank with him in little bars and heard him loudly vociferating in the small hours of the morning, tell us that he sometimes lost all self-control, flew into ungovernable rages and even struck the women whom he loved. Does this truly matter? Is it even truly *true*? What his works prove conclusively is that he was, above all, a master; and all aesthetic mastery calls for self-mastery on the artist's part. Amedeo, the man, may have been shaking with cold, despair and the effects of drink as he roved the boulevards of Montparnasse, but his hand never shook upon the white expanse of paper or canvas he was working on.

There is no denying that Modigliani's brief existence flamed itself away in a series of mad caprices and drinking bouts, in dissipation and disaster. He was almost always penniless, drunk, driven before an evil wind of destiny. Most of his contemporaries saw in him an ineffectual reactionary, a conservative Bohemian who was trying to effect an impossible fusion of tradition with audacity, of serenity with exacerbated emotionalism; as, in fact, a charming, helpless innocent. Nothing could have been farther from the truth. Modigliani has more in common with one of those exiled princes disguised as beggars whom we read of in fairy-tales, and who at the story's end, casting off their rags, triumphantly ascend the throne.

One may be sometimes tempted to smile, a shade superiorly, at the naïve lyricism and Italian exuberance of some of the aphorisms Amedeo jotted down in the margins of his drawings. Personally I admit to being frankly moved by the lines he wrote one day under one of his loveliest pencil sketches: *La vita è un dono: dei pochi ai molti: di coloro che sanno e che hanno a coloro che non sanno e che non hanno.* (Life is a gift; from the few to the many; from those who know and have to those who do not know and have not.) Modigliani knew, Modigliani had everything, and throughout his life bestowed it lavishly on all. Let us try, then, to appraise, to understand and to esteem his work at the highest level, that of the Masters.

Amedeo Modigliani in 1909. Photograph.

Biography and Background

With a few exceptions, it is extremely difficult to date the events of Modigliani's life with any precision. He never dated his letters and the witness accounts of his contemporaries are often contradictory. Hence the difficulties in compiling the biographical outline given below, which, however, we believe to be substantially correct.

1884 Birth of Amedeo, fourth child of Flaminio Modigliani and Eugénie Garsin, at Leghorn, Italy, on July 12. The Modiglianis were an old Jewish family long established in the village of that name, south of Rome. Amedeo's grandfather had been a banker in Rome, which he left to settle at Leghorn, where his youngest son Flaminio was director of a "banco" (broker's office). The Garsins were a family of Sephardim Jews from Marseilles.

1880-1895 Giovanni Fattori paints in Tuscany.

1882 Triple Alliance (Austria, Germany, Italy).

1883 Publication of Nietzsche's *Thus Spake Zarathustra*.

1884 Founding in Paris of the Société des Indépendants: Seurat, Signac, Cross, Redon and others.

1886 Fattori put in charge of the finishing course for advanced art students at the Academy of Florence.
Publication of Nietzsche's *Beyond Good and Evil*.

1894 Publication of D'Annunzio's *Triumph of Death*.

1895 Amedeo falls ill with pleurisy. Schooling at the Liceo of Leghorn.

1895 Cézanne exhibition at Ambroise Vollard's gallery in Paris.

1896 Abyssinian war. Italy seizes Eritrea and Somaliland.
D'Annunzio publishes a sensational article calling upon Italian writers to create a new literature, European in scope.

1898 Amedeo has an attack of typhoid fever, followed by pulmonary complications. He nevertheless qualifies for his diploma at the Liceo, after enrolling in Micheli's class at the Leghorn School of Fine Arts.

1898 Birth of Jeanne Hébuterne (April 6).

1900 D'Annunzio elected by ultra-conservative elements to the Italian legislature, where he is nicknamed "the Representative of Beauty."
Picasso's first visit to Paris.
Benedetto Croce publishes his *Historical Materialism and Marxist Economics*.

1901 Another attack of tuberculosis. Visits Florence, Rome, Naples and Capri.

1901 Death of Toulouse-Lautrec. Picasso's Blue Period.

1902 May: Modigliani enrolls at the School of Fine Arts, Florence.

1902 Lautrec retrospective exhibition in Paris at Durand-Ruel's and the Salon des Indépendants.
D'Annunzio publishes his play *Francesca da Rimini*.

1903 March: Modigliani enrolls at the School of Fine Arts, Venice.

1904 Pirandello publishes his novel *The Late Mattia Pascal*.
Cézanne exhibits 42 canvases at the Salon d'Automne, Paris.
Constantin Brancusi comes to Paris.

1905 Pascin comes to Paris.

Late 1905 or early 1906 Modigliani arrives in Paris. Lives in the Rue Caulaincourt, near the Bateau-Lavoir, in Montmartre.

1906 The critic Louis Vauxcelles coins the term "Fauvism" at the Salon d'Automne. Gino Severini and Juan Gris arrive in Paris. Rehabilitation of Captain Dreyfus.
Riots in Paris after the passing of the Separation Law dividing Church from State.

1907 Modigliani becomes a member of the Société des Indépendants.

1907 Cézanne memorial exhibition at the Salon d'Automne.

1908 At the Salon des Indépendants Modigliani exhibits "The Jewess" and four other canvases. In October or November he meets Dr Paul Alexandre.

1908 Speaking mockingly of painting in "little cubes," Vauxcelles coins the name "Cubism." Matisse begins collecting African carvings.

1909 Modigliani moves to the Cité Falguière, in Montparnasse, where he becomes friendly with Brancusi. In the autumn he returns to Leghorn where he seems to have concentrated on sculpture.

1909 Execution of the anarchist Francisco Ferrer in Barcelona.
Publication of the first Futurist Manifesto.
Utrillo exhibits at the Salon d'Automne.

1910 Back in Paris, Modigliani lives and works (chiefly at sculpture) at the Cité Falguière. At the Salon des Indépendants he exhibits "The Beggar Woman," "The Cellist" and "The Beggar of Leghorn."

1910 Publication of D'Annunzio's novel *Forse che sì, forse che no.*
Première of Stravinsky's *Fire Bird* in Paris.
Manifesto of Futurist Painting published in Milan.
Chagall and Mondrian come to Paris.

1911 Italy annexes Tripolitania. Chirico comes to Paris.

1912 Soutine comes to Paris, where he attempts to commit suicide.

1913 Summer at Leghorn (?)

1913 Apollinaire publishes *Les peintres cubistes.*

1914 Love affair with the English poetess Beatrice Hastings. Meets Leopold Zborowski. The Paris dealer Paul Guillaume begins to buy his canvases.

1914 Pascin is in England when war is declared and sails for the United States.

1917 July: Modigliani meets Jeanne Hébuterne.

1917 Tristan Tzara publishes Dada I and Dada II in Zurich.
Matisse settles at Nice.

1918 Modigliani exhibition at Berthe Weill's gallery in Paris.

1918 Death of Guillaume Apollinaire.

1918-1919 A stay at Nice with the Survages. Jeanne Hébuterne gives birth to a daughter, christened Jeanne, on November 29, 1918.

1919-1920 Modigliani lives in the Rue de la Grande Chaumière in Montparnasse.

1919 Death of Renoir at Cagnes, on the Riviera, December 3.

1920 Modigliani dies of tuberculosis at the Hôpital de la Charité, Paris, January 25. Jeanne Hébuterne commits suicide, January 26.

Café du Dôme, Paris. Period photograph.

Index of Names

PRINTED BY
IRL IMPRIMERIES RÉUNIES LAUSANNE S.A.

BINDING BY
MAYER & SOUTTER, RENENS/LAUSANNE

Printed in Switzerland